FURNITURE

Architects' and Designers' Originals

Carol Soucek King, Ph.D.

ARCHITECTURE & INTERIOR DESIGN LIBRARY

An Imprint of
PBC International, Inc.

Distributor to the book trade in the United States and Canada

Rizzoli International Publications Inc.
300 Park Avenue South
New York, NY 10010

Distributor to the art trade in the United States and Canada

PBC International, Inc.
One School Street
Glen Cove, NY 11542

Distributor throughout the rest of the world

Hearst Books International
1350 Avenue of the Americas
New York, NY 10019

Library Of Congress Cataloging–in–Publication Data

King, Carol Soucek
    Furniture : architects' and designers' originals / by Carol Soucek King.
        p.   cm. — (Architectural and interior design library)
    Includes index.
    ISBN 0–86636–292–4
    1. Architect-designed furniture. 2. Furniture design.
3. Furniture designers—Quotations. I. Title. II. Series
NK2702.K56   1994   94-7804
749.2 ' 0498—dc20   CIP

CAVEAT– Information in this text is believed accurate, and will pose no problem for the student or casual reader.
However, the author was often constrained by information contained in signed release forms, information that
could have been in error or not included at all. Any misinformation (or lack of information) is the result of failure
in these attestations. The author has done whatever is possible to insure accuracy.

Color separation by
Fine Arts Repro House Co., Ltd., H.K.

Printing and binding by
Toppan Printing Co., Ltd., H.K.

10 9 8 7 6 5 4 3 2 1

Printed in China

To those who inspire design excellence...

To those who achieve it...

And to those who support the quest!

TABLE OF CONTENTS

Preface

What special perspective do those entrusted with the creation of entire environments bring to the design of the individual objects within? It was my interest in that question which led to the following visits with some of the world's leading architects and interior designers who are also known for their design of furniture. I asked each of them these three questions:

How does being an architect or interior designer affect your perspective as a furniture designer?

What to you is the most important: the design itself, or its fabrication, or its function?

What is the designer's responsibility in relation to ergonomics? Ecology? Longevity?

We are living in a time when the people of all countries are having to readdress their economic situations. They are rethinking their influence on the environment and, for the first time in their lives, inquiring about how everything they buy is made, used and discarded. They are reconsidering how, rather than suffer from increased competition from foreign sources, they might take advantage of the opportunities made possible by today's exponentially expanding international trade. A result of all these revolutions of thought and action is a growing awareness that, to be excellent, design must answer to a universe of values. In terms of residential furniture design, those who already are involved with the concerns of their clients' personal needs, tastes and living situations have much to bring to the design of the pieces on which they sit, serve dinner, store their goods and go to sleep.

This is a time when being "different just to be different" is considered altogether unprincipled, when the way an item is made is being scrutinized with as much rigor as its appearance, and when possessions are being asked as never before to perform as advertised. Yet at the same time, feeling numbed by a growing similarity among products made available to a mass market, consumers are in avid quest of things even slightly unique as well as products that will help them express their own individuality.

Awakened by the renaissance of the decorative arts and by the abundance of materials and finishes and techniques now available from around the world, people will no longer accept furniture which is well-made but dull. And even if furniture does serve its intended function, if it does so without also contributing to the richness of human experience, without paying heed to that of which history has made us aware, the consumer will not...cannot...feel satisfied. After all, the objects that surround us are testimony to who we are and, because we interact with them daily, play a role in defining who we are.

Everything in the universe is related, and those that grasp this can be giants. Viewed in this light, furniture is not simply material merchandise; it symbolizes our past, present and future. It can work for or against our attitudes and philosophies. It can ignite our sense of adventure and joy. It can elevate our existence. This, perhaps more than any other aspect, was my incentive in capturing the thoughts and creativity of the designers featured in this book. To hear from them about their involvement with their art is a captivating, intense, exhilarating exploration into the effect of man on many diverse but interrelated aspects of the built and natural environment. Taken together, the compilation of their remarks expresses countless connections between virtually everything known to man, relating design on a galactic scale to design on a most intimate, human scale.

Such commentaries are not mere addenda to the designs of these professionals. Such mental excursions have a vitality that is carried throughout their own work and outward to others, sharpening analyses of design's every aspect and, indeed, magnifying the value of good design. The architects and interior designers included in this volume have all been hungry to reveal goals attained and explain others less understood, to transcend their solitary tracings and expand upon their former blueprints. They have elucidated the thought of furniture design as a crucible for the refinement of architecture and design. Most importantly, they have been able to identify those qualities that not only distinguish their furniture design and its fabrication but also, and most importantly, that infuse it with a sense of spirit.

—C.S.K.

Introduction

An Interview with Dr. Franco Arquati

As president of the Milan Furniture Fair, Dr. Franco Arquati is not only involved with the production of furniture internationally, but also has an intimate knowledge of the manufacturers and designers in his own country. Since Italy is the leading exporter of furniture in the world, it seemed particularly appropriate to seek his comments on the state of the residential furniture market today and how, based on his experience, and especially that of the Italians, its strengths might be emphasized.

Dr. Franco Arquati
President (1990-1993), Salone del Mobile di Milano

CSK: *How does being an architect or interior designer affect the furniture designer's perspective?*

FA: Furniture design has a high-profile presence in all the places where young designers are trained, such as design schools and colleges, faculties of architecture, not to mention design consultancies. As a result, in typically Italian fashion, there is not one way of training to be a furniture designer, but several.

The major manufacturers call upon the talents of the leading names on the Italian and international design scene, while also being attentive to the portfolios sent in by some of the less well-established names. Another way in which young designers can attract attention to themselves is via the great many design competitions we have here in Italy. Many of these are sponsored by the large number of Italian design publications, which play an enormously important role in spreading the word.

On a technical level, a furniture designer needs to have an in-depth knowledge of furniture history, as well as to be well acquainted with the materials and the leading manufacturing processes. Needless to say, the furniture designer also needs to know what the "state of the art" currently is, to avoid running the risk of copying ideas that are already in use, or of working on others which have run their course.

Clearly a furniture designer needs to have a good general background, as well as an interest and aptitude for psychological and social inquiry, along with endless amounts of imagination and creativity. For, at the end of the day, designing furniture means working in a field that draws from a vast heritage, in which it has often been thought that all opportunities for forms, materials and functions have been exhausted.

CSK: *What is most important in furniture design today: the design itself, or its fabrication, or its function?*

FA: In the Italian furniture sector, the concept of design is very much closer to the accepted meaning than in others. A good design is one that brings together good looks, fitness for the purpose, and precision-perfect use of the industrial manufacturing process. Thus, we do not tend to consider things that are beautiful and yet do not have a market application, or that are difficult, costly, and time-consuming to manufacture, as being good designs.

The worldwide success of Italian design—and bear in mind that Italy is the world's Number One furniture exporter—is the outcome of such an approach, which is a winning formula from a variety of points of view. This approach to design is made possible by the fact that, in Italy, we have some thirty-five thousand small furniture manufacturing units which can also draw on the storehouse of specialist skills provided by an even greater number of artisans.

This unique approach to manufacturing, where companies are working to some degree in competition and to another in collaboration, leads us to be able to have what we in Italian call the *ingegnerizzazione del prototipo,* in other words where we can examine and experiment on the prototype at all angles to ensure that we end up with the ideal product.

CSK: *What is the responsibility of the designer in relation to ergonomics? Ecology? Longevity?*

FA: A furniture designer is called upon to design a product that looks attractive and innovative, can be manufactured in a cost-effective fashion, and is fit for its purpose. In other words, what we want is something that is useful and is not the result of the latest fashion whim. There are, clearly, companies—those catering to an upmarket clientele, for example—for whom price is not a major consideration, and whose priority is to ensure that the finished product looks sufficiently exclusive, with money no object. At the other extreme, we find companies launching products whose only innovative feature is the fact that they are inexpensive.

At the present time, though, there is the feeling about that designers are being asked to prioritize value-for-money and durability. The result is that in Italy—as elsewhere—the drive for "innovation for innovation's sake" has slowed somewhat. Designers are now being called upon to address the challenge of masterminding highly innovative products, which can leave the competition standing and stimulate people who are not in the mood to buy to part with their money. Vogueishness should be kept to a minimum so that these pieces do not go out of fashion. Some observers have called this the crisis of the design world. In my view, though, this is an outstanding opportunity for designers to make the most of their creativity.

CSK: *How would you assess the international mix of furniture available today and the chance of cross-cultural influences?*

FA: As far as the current mix of products available is concerned, I would say that the answer is contained in what I have already said. In the sense that the "overall" approach to design, which is the hallmark of Italian design, involves a kind of "give" and "take" position. On the "giving" side, we have the strengths that an individual country's design world has. In the case of Italy, this is the name, for example. Then, on the "take" side, there is what the designer needs to assimilate about the other country, the aspects that need to be accommodated to create a product suitable for that country. If I may take the example of picture frames, then we can see a clear demonstration of what I am saying. Different materials and different styles are specific to specific market needs.

Thus, we can say that operating on the world stage entails taking best advantage of economics of scale, managing one's finances, monitoring exchange-rate fluctuations, and making the most of these. At the same time, it means observing one's markets and ensuring that the products being designed are fit for those markets. These are difficult tasks, requiring time and commitment, with no cutting of corners allowed. The rewards are there, though, and over and above monetary gain, help to raise one's profile and enhance one's reputation.

CSK: *What are your observations on the importance of the home today and its relationship to the health of the home furnishings market?*

FA: Housing comes very close to food in terms of people's priorities. While people may now be buying fewer, and less expensive, pieces of furniture, people still love their homes. Thus the future of the furniture market is assured.

This does lead to a contradictory process—at least it does in Europe anyway—whereby furniture is seen as a consumer durable which is important and which people are willing to spend considerable sums on, but is a purchase which people can postpone if they are feeling the pinch financially. In Italy, as elsewhere, 1993 was a very negative year economically, with domestic demand falling more than ten percent. This has left more than a few businesses in difficulty. Luckily, for Italian exporters, the devaluation of the lire against the US dollar and the deutsche mark has improved their fortunes.

However, it is undoubtedly true that consumer crises stimulate a turnaround in the market. For a start, in a crisis period, people who are now finding they have less to spend on going out and going on holiday, for example, are spending more time at home. In the process, they rediscover what we might call "domestic pleasures" and this then stimulates their desire to make their homes more welcoming and more comfortable. This trend came through loud and clear at the last Salone del Mobile.

TABLES

Eero Aarnio

Alison Wright

Rand Elliott

Robert Frank McAlpine

James F. Jereb

Richard Himmel

Pucci De Rossi

Laurie Ann Clemans

Eva Jiricna

Andrée Putman

Geoffrey Scott

Ward Bennett

Paul Tuttle

Robert A.M. Stern

John Chan

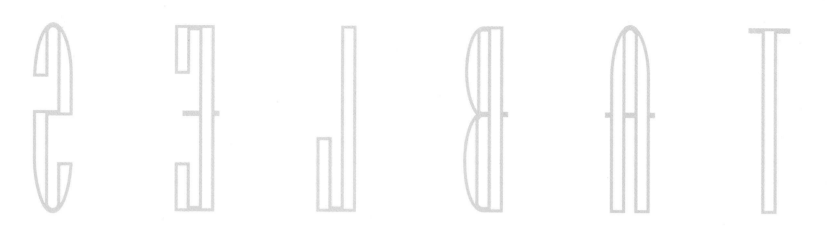

Peter Wooding

Margaret Helfand

Samuel Botero

Leavitt/Weaver

Elyse B. Lacher

Oscar Tusquets Blanca

Carlos and Gerard Pascal

Joseph Alcasar Terrell

Antonio Citterio

Bradley Rath

Sherle Wagner

Mark Simon

Eric Owen Moss

Sally Sirkin Lewis

Eero Aarnio

With the recent debut of his Screw Table, Eero Aarnio has been turning heads as he has done ever since setting up his studio in Helsinki in 1962. By 1963 he had designed the Ball Chair, the fiberglass

material and shape of which were a complete novelty for the furniture industry of that time. The same was true when he designed the Pastilli Chair four years later. These two models, followed by the Tomato Chair in 1971, gave him international stature with his works soon being found in numerous collections and museums around the world. Today they can be seen at the Museum of Modern Art, New York; the Vitra Design Museum, Weil a. Rhein; Centre Georges Pompidou, Paris; and the Victoria and Albert Museum, London.

Educated at The School of Applied Art in Helsinki as both interior and industrial designer, he says it is not possible to separate the two fields anymore than one can separate architecture from interior design or function from aesthetics.

"Architecture, design and art...they are not separate things. A design's function is its brain, its appearance is its heart."

Copacabana Table. Designed by Eero Aarnio, 1991. Fiberglass. Available in black, white, red, green and yellow. Manufactured by Adelta Oy. Photography by Harri Kosonen

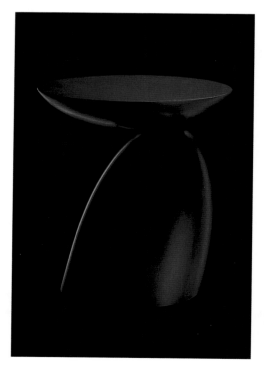

Parabel Table. Designed by Eero Aarnio, 1994. Birchwood. Manufactured by Adelta Oy. Photography by Harri Kosonen

Screw Table. *Designed by Eero Aarnio,*
1991. Fiberglass. Available in black,
white, red, green, yellow, gray metallic,
anthracite metallic. Manufactured by
Adelta Oy.
Photography by Harri Kosonen

Alison Wright

A lison Wright is an architect based in Los Angeles, where she opened Alison Wright-Architects in 1987. She was a faculty member at Otis Art Institute of Parsons School of Design from 1987 to 1990, and she was director of design for Levin & Associates from 1980 to 1987. She held the position of designer/job captain with Group Arcon in 1980.

In association with Levin & Associates, Wright received a 1987 American Institute of Architects Honor Award for her design of McDonalds at the Fine Arts Building, Los Angeles; and she received a 1988 Urban League Institute award for the Downtown Women's Center, Los Angeles. In 1991 Wright received the Los Angeles Conservancy Preservation Award for

her design for the Seventh Street Produce Market.

Wright studied French literature at the Université de Strasbourg from 1975 to 1976. She received a Bachelor of Science degree in Architecture from the University of Southern California in 1980, and a Bachelor of Architecture degree from the Southern California Institute of Architecture in 1981.

"As an architect, furniture design and architectural space and volume are complementary elements. Some furniture items should take a secondary role and allow the space to dominate. Others should act as foci, demanding primary attention which slowly allows one to understand the space better. The Trapezoidal Table as used in the Manhattan Beach residence shown here gives the first clues that a non-rectilinear space exists above it."

"Every item created has its own role; one may be spiritual, another physical. The intent of the piece governs whether the design itself, the fabrication or function is the preeminent factor in its resolution. For the Trapezoidal Dining Table, all three aspects were significant. However, the design itself was most important. The table was to be responsive to a trapezoidal space visible from a two-story volume."

"Different furniture pieces have differing roles and as such their role governs the responsibility that each item has in terms of the environment, its users or its function. For example, an art piece such as Merit Oppenheim's fur teacup does not serve the same function as Frank Lloyd Wright's teacups for the Imperial Hotel. With that distinction made, every object has an obligation to respond to its users, function and the environment. However, this responsiveness may be achieved in many ways and may or may not be primary in determining its form."

Trapezoidal Dining Table. *Designed by Alison Wright, 1992. Bent diamond plate steel and clear glass. Custom design through Alison Wright-Architects. Photography by Grey Crawford*

Rand Elliott

When Rand Elliott premiered The E-Squared Collection, he seemed clearly to be reflecting his refreshingly experimental, highly developed understanding of form and light seen throughout his architecture and interior design.

The genesis of the collection occurred in 1987, when Elliott invented and patented a process that transforms clear acrylic into a textured material that reflects and holds light. As the effect resembles ice, he named it "Icing." Its quality of an almost ghostly translucence also serves as a visual metaphor for the ghost towns in his native Oklahoma, after which Elliott named each piece: Turn, Jet, Curl, Hoopville and Bowlegs which was named for Seminole chief Billy Bowlegs.... Now, after creating numerous additional pieces for the collection, Elliott comments that the influence of his other design work is definitely present.

"The furniture is a building with legs," he says. "Furniture is a building with small inhabitants. Furniture is form put to use. Furniture is a single gesture in contact with human body parts."

And designing that gesture he says is his favorite part of the creative process.

> *"The idea/concept/inspiration is the most rewarding. Fabrication becomes anticlimactic. I have already built it in my mind. I already know what it will be. The idea is lasting."*

> *"The responsibility of the designer is to do something beautiful that functions appropriately for the intended use while at the same time redefining that intended use."*

Curl. *Designed by Rand Elliott, 1990. Fabricated by Phil Bewley. Available through the designer. Namesake: An Oklahoma ghost town that existed in Blaine County from June 4, 1901 to October 25, 1901. Named for G. T. Curl, Blaine County longtime resident. Photography by Bob Shimer, Hedrich-Blessing*

Jet. *Designed by Rand Elliott, 1990. Fabricated by Phil Bewley. Available through the designer. A low, round coffee table with a cutout V and a large fold across on edge. Namesake: An Oklahoma territorial town established in Alfalfa County on June 28, 1894. Named for W. M. Jett, miller and first postmaster. Photography by Bob Shimer, Hedrich-Blessing*

Turn. Designed by Rand Elliott, 1990. Fabricated by Phil Bewley. Available through the designer. Elliott's original Iced piece, a sleek cigarette table. Namesake: An Oklahoma ghost town that existed in Pottawatomie County from January 25, 1892 to October 29, 1895. Named for the town's first postmaster, Christopher C. Turner. Photography by Bob Shimer, Hedrich-Blessing

Bowlegs. Designed by Rand Elliott, 1990. Fabricated by Phil Bewley. Available through the designer. A side table that fits a 90 degree corner and leans against the wall, touching the floor at a single point. Namesake: An Oklahoma town established April 23, 1927 in Seminole County. Named for Billy Bowlegs, a Seminole chief. Photography by Bob Shimer, Hedrich-Blessing

Hoopville. Designed by Rand Elliott, 1990. Fabricated by Phil Bewley. Available through the designer. A table that gains its balance by leaning against the wall. Namesake: An Oklahoma ghost town that existed in Major County from January 7, 1908 to January 29, 1913. Formerly known as Estelle, it later became Sherman. Twine, designed in 1989 by Elliott, is a wall-mounted flower vessel. Namesake: An Oklahoma territorial ghost town that existed in Muskogee County from March 28, 1902 to November 1904. Named for early-day resident W. H. Twine. Photography by Bob Shimer, Hedrich-Blessing

Robert Frank McAlpine

"*N*urturing"..."compassionate"..."soulful." These words grace conversations with Robert Frank McAlpine about his architectural and interior design practice which he conducts from his French châteauesque Sabel Mansion in Montgomery, Alabama. And in discussions regarding the materials used in his new furniture line, he describes steel as "very gymnastic" and wood as "more heartfelt and resonant."

"Only through the use of steel can you achieve the delicacy of a French leg that is more delicate than the French wooden leg itself," he says. "The steel legs on these tables are inspired by the tension of an animal's leg. In opposition, the wooden tops of these tables, with their slightly splayed sides and heavy proportion of their edges, look very monolithic."

The veneer of both tabletops is divided to highlight the placement of the legs. In the larger table, the pattern originates from the two focal points of the ellipse, McAlpine's favorite shape "because of its infinite grace from any angle combined with a sense of aggression and slightly directional nature."

"Very often my designs for furniture are not as willful as they are efforts to solve a design problem, to create a piece to complete an interior that the marketplace does not have.

"Designing houses draws on many mixed origins. In this search for compatible souls among various styles I sometimes find compassionate relationships between seemingly dissimilar models as well as materials. Such is the relationship between wood and steel."

"In designing furniture, I consider for myself the design and its function to be more important than the fabrication, for these are the two things over which I have most control. The testimony of the grace of a piece is its utility."

"As an architect it is maturity that yields longevity, and longevity covers all aspects of the architect's responsibility. Ergonomics is crucial (if the designer can keep it straight) in that it is the grace that the piece allows the human form that will vouch for its continued audience. The piece itself is secondary to the image made when it is occupied."

French Profile Table. *Designed by Robert Frank McAlpine, 1990. Manufactured by Studio Amerika Limited. Steel and purple heart with natural finish. Represented by Jerry Pair. Photography by Billy Marks*

Walden Table. *Designed by Robert Frank McAlpine, 1989. Manufactured by Studio Amerika Limited. Steel and red mahogany with ebonized ash top. Represented by Jerry Pair. Photography by Billy Marks*

James F. Jereb

*J*ames F. Jereb, Ph.D., the Antonio Gaudi of Santa Fe, creates with his hands what his imagination sees and his spirit intuits. Even within and without his own home and Tribal Design studio, expressions indigenous to the Third World cultures of his interests and travels are translated visually through his personal understanding of what he calls the "international collective unconscious."

Jereb owns and operates Tribal Design which incorporates design consultation for interiors and exteriors and commissioned work in bas-relief and sculpture of adobe, tile and mixed media. He has a Ph.D. degree in art history and is currently writing a book titled *Al Baraka/Arts and Crafts of Morocco,* to be published by Thames & Hudson Ltd. in 1995. He is also curator of a traveling exhibition with the same title.

"In my design, most of the furniture is architectural and site specific. I think you have to have the sensitivity of both the architect and the interior designer to make furniture."

"For me, the design is part of the hands-on process coupled with the fabrication of the object. Since most of my pieces are built by hand, they cannot really be separated from the design. The conception of the design is important as the first step, but I guess if I had to choose, the fabrication is the highlight of that creative source."

"I think designers, as do all people, have a definite responsibility to be concerned citizens of this world and to allow this concern to be reflected in their art...not in a rote fashion but in a meaningful way appropriate to their creativity. For myself, I use natural materials and recycled tile, mirror and other items as much as I can. My new direction includes mud plaster slips and alternative materials such as pumice crete and recycled glass."

Interior Alcove/Shelf. *Designed and built by James F. Jereb, 1992. Special order through Tribal Design. Shelf of recycled wood. Archway constructed of adobe with plaster, painted with acrylic and gold leaf with mixed media. Measures 6 feet long x 7 feet high. Photography by Lynn Lown*

Shamanistic Dance. *Dining room table with six chairs, designed and built by James F. Jereb, 1993. Special order through Tribal Design. Mixed Media, painted surface with various glazes, pattern includes lightning flash for each place setting. Each part of the reconstructed vintage chairs has a different totem on back panel and imitation fur seats. Photography by Lynn Lown*

Richard Himmel

*A*n irreverent, outspoken critic voyeur of his own mixed media lifestyle, Richard Himmel has been actively interior designing for more than forty years. Although the main part of his time is spent in decorating apartments and homes across this country and Europe, he has been the interior designer of many major hotel and motel installations, country clubs, corporate aircraft, railroad cars, yachts, restaurants, banks, private clubs and retail stores.

Himmel has also received great recognition for his outstanding design of restaurant and table appointments and settings for them. In addition to his regular design business, Himmel is a specialist in the design of upholstered furniture. He has designed for Dods-Murdick Transitional Furniture, Baker Furniture Company, Interior Crafts, Inc., and most recently a new collection of soft seating for his own showroom in Chicago's Merchandise Mart, Richard Himmel Antique and Decorative Furniture. He is also known for his knowledge of period styles and his reinterpretations of period furniture.

He has been the recipient of numerous prestigious awards for his contributions to the interior design industry as well as for his design excellence, including the highest award his peers in the United States could bestow—the Designer of Distinction award presented to him in 1992 by the American Society of Interior Designers.

"Shopping with clients both domestically and internationally has given me the best perspective toward designing furniture. I know the furniture market and I know the antique market. I design furniture I know I'll never find."

"Like eighteenth-century French furniture, quality and design should be equal partners. If a piece is the transitory home for a chilled martini, that's function enough."

"My responsibility as a designer is to extend design as a fashion business; one needs to be keenly aware of trends while trying to produce 'timelessness.' It is both the burden and the raison d'être to make furniture and objects that can't be held to a circa date."

De Gaulle Desk. *Designed by Richard Himmel, 1990. Antique faux silver finish, available in custom finishes. Available through Richard Himmel Antique and Decorative Furniture. Photography by Christopher Barrett/Kingfish Photography*

Ectoskeletal Commode Chaudronnier. *A collaborative work by John Himmel and artist/artisan Evan Lewis, 1993. (Artist Evan Lewis, with whom Himmel has frequently collaborated, makes outdoor kinetic sculptures which move by the power of the wind and, in recent pieces, make sounds as they move.) Formed iron-hammered copper and found wood. Available through Richard Himmel Antique and Decorative Furniture. Shown with Piranesi trumeau designed by Richard Himmel, 1993. Upper insert from Series Italian Urns by Piranesi. Photography by Christopher Barrett/Kingfish Photography*

Pucci De Rossi

"*I* am primarily an artist and sculptor, and I approach interior design and the design of furniture as if they are works of art," says this Verona native, now residing in Paris. His one-of-a-kind art furniture has found permanent residence in the Louvre's Museum of Decorative Arts and the

Museum of Modern Art/Pompidou Center, as well as in homes in many countries, some of which have interiors entirely "sculpted" by Pucci De Rossi.

De Rossi's artistic career began in the early 1970s when he studied under sculptor H. Brooks Walker. After his first personal exhibit at the Galerie Art 3 in Paris in 1973, he began participating in exhibits in Italy from Milan to Venice.

By 1977 the artist had emigrated from Italy to Paris, where he continued to participate in numerous group exhibits and was honored in 1980 with his own show in Paris's Galerie Caroline Corre. Broadening his base to include designing theater decor, De Rossi continued dedicating himself to creating one-of-a-kind functional art.

"I begin the process of designing a piece of furniture by experimenting with volume," he says. "The challenge is to arrive at a balance between the negative and positive spaces involved in a three-dimensional piece of sculpture. The volume of the positive space has to be visually light, graceful and fluid. When combining different shapes, they have to speak the same language and be logical."

"I don't consider my work geometrical but, unconsciously, I seem to gravitate to those shapes: circles and squares. For me, they tell a story.

"The most difficult part of designing furniture is integrating the two parts so that they balance each other, give support to the weight of a top, and are stable.

"The challenge always is combining the aesthetic with the practical."

Battista. *Designed by Pucci De Rossi, 1988. Manufactured in Los Angeles by H. Dolin Stuart and available through designer showrooms around the United States, and through Neotu Gallery in Paris. Instead of placing two distinct profiles in the perpendicular position typical of pieces, the designer angles them here for the first time. This side table is made of ½ inch steel in a variety of finishes and holds glass tops up to 24 inches. Photography by Cameron Carothers*

Vizir. *Designed by Pucci De Rossi, 1989. Manufactured in Los Angeles by H. Dolin Stuart, and available through designer showrooms around the United States, and through Neotu Gallery in Paris. Inspired by lyrical arabesque forms, this console is made of ½ inch steel in a variety of finishes and holds glass and marble tops up to 6 feet in length. Photography by Cameron Carothers*

Laurie Ann Clemans

*L*aurie Ann Clemans started designing and producing custom furniture in 1984 after seeing unusual art furniture at Art et Industrie in New York and then the Memphis collection. "I was propelled to look at furni-

ture in a new, sculptural way," says the Walnut Creek, California-based Clemans who, until then, had been working exclusively as an art director/designer in graphic design and advertising. Just two years later, however, she won a Progressive Architecture International Furniture Design Award, and a short time later her work was exhibited at the International Design Center in New York, the Boston Design Center and appeared on NBC's "Today Show." In 1993 she participated in an installation at the Thread Waxing Space in New York City.

She continues to design one-of-a-kind furniture and accessories for both interiors and the garden. Now however she has expanded her business to include interior design and is currently working on a production line of home accessories.

"By spending seven years designing furniture before expanding into interior design, I have a unique perspective on the two disciplines.

"Through furniture design, I explore an unlimited range of materials and possibilities. I draw inspiration from fashion, jewelry, costume, history, art and nature. This broad vision is possible because my pieces become focal points.

"Through interior design, I am concerned with how elements work with each other and the total environment. I utilize my passionate, eclectic perspective. Yet all the while I am taking into account my client's particular requirements and point of view. Interior design affords me the opportunity to create personal living spaces that are easy to live with!...and to more successfully design furniture that works within those spaces."

"When I began designing furniture, I gave myself these parameters to work toward: The pieces must be exquisitely designed, meticulously crafted, timeless, and absolutely functional. I still work the same way. Design, fabrication and function are equally important in my design process."

Birds in Cages: Escape! *Designed by Laurie Ann Clemans, 1988. Fabricated by Laurie Ann Clemans Design. Rust finished forged and wrought steel base. Hollywood stone top.*
Photography by Alexander Vertikoff

"As furniture designers and as human beings, we are responsible for the work we produce—to our clients and to the environment. For our clients, we must create work that is comfortable and practical ergonomically, that is structurally sound, that will be there for our children's children! For our designs and for the environment, we must choose natural resources that are not endangered, develop processes that are not toxic, use discretion in the quantities we produce. Continued personal vigilance within these areas is of supreme importance to us all."

Diamond Jubilee Cocktail Table.

Designed by Laurie Ann Clemans, 1984.

Fabricated by Laurie Ann Clemans

Design. Black lacquer, facetted Lucite,

Austrian foil-back rhinestones.

Photography by Henrik Kam

Eva Jiricna

*E*va Jiricna has established herself as a unique yet versatile architect whose talented team can be relied upon to deliver work of the very highest calibre, usually within very tight schedules and budget constraints.

Eva Jiricna Architects Limited, headquartered in London, has gained a high-profile reputation for retail and commercial design, fit-outs of night-

clubs and restaurants, "one off" residential conversions, and systems design. Growing client awareness of the quality of work and attention to detail which the practice brings to bear on its projects, together with originality of approach, has resulted in the type, scope and size of commissions being broadened and diversified.

Born in Czechoslavakia, Jiricna received a degree in architecture/engineering from Prague University and a postgraduate degree from Prague Academy of Fine Arts. She moved to England in 1968 and, not able to return after that summer's momentous events, continued working in London with a number of practices until establishing her own firm in 1984. It became a limited company in 1992, with longstanding colleague Jon Tollit becoming fellow director.

"Whether an architect or designer, the principle remains the same: to understand the problem and design an object to suit. The process 'to design' is identical whether one is dealing with a building or a piece of furniture."

"Function, appearance, fabrication, material selection, maintenance, lifespan, etc. are all equally important in the design process. If one is given priority over another, I feel it is impossible to achieve what is called 'good design.' "

"The designer carries all the reponsibility for the design, which does not mean that he or she is incapable of making mistakes, as we all know. The only problems that a designer is not responsible for are changes, if any, introduced without approval during the process of production."

Dining Table. *Designed by Eva Jiricna, 1981. Perforated metal. Custom design for a private residence in London.*

When not in use, the table folds up against the wall. The seats, which double as adjustable tables, have no backrests and are provided with an inflatable cushion. The bench on the other side is clad in industrial studded rubber and divides the dining area from the seating enclosure. Photography by Richard Bryant/Arcaid

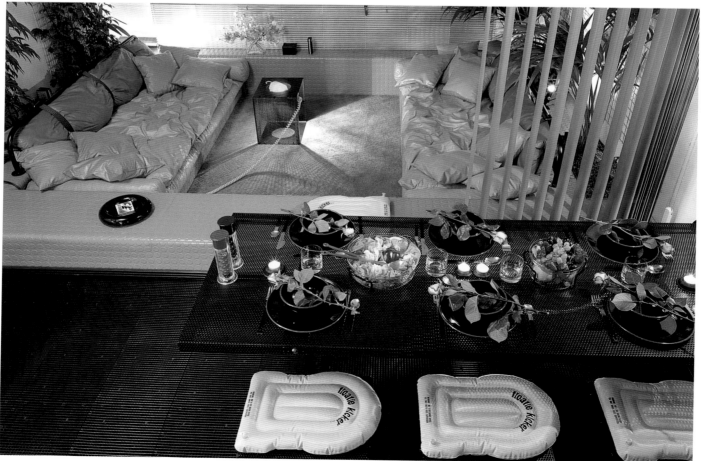

Andrée Putman

PHOTOGRAPHY BY ROLAND BEAUFRE

*A*ndrée Putman dedicated The Ecart Group, which she founded in Paris in 1978, "to the art of living realized through scrupulous attention to detail, the control of light, and a commitment to timeless aesthetic values that transcend the bounds of fashion." This philosophy guides the three departments of the group in the practice of their respective disciplines.

Ecart S.A. is composed of creative experts who specialize in interior and product design. The agency's diversified design portfolio ranges from hotels to boutiques, from corporate headquarters to private homes, and from museums to government offices.

Ecart International promotes and preserves works dating from the turn of the century, reissuing furniture and objects created by designers such as Eileen Gray, Jean Michel Frank, Mariano Fortuny...Pursuing its role as a pioneer in the design field, Ecart International also promotes the new creations of Ecart S.A. and other contemporary talents.

"Of course, being involved with the design of entire interiors affects your approach to designing furniture, and it especially has a great impact on the way you decide on scale, as you are much more familiar with space when you practice as an interior designer."

"In designing furniture, both the design and the function are most important. Of course, the fabrication is important, but that depends on all the rest."

3 Suisses Table. *Designed by Andrée Putman, 1993. Distributed by 3 Suisses. Metal, epoxy paint. Color: orange, white, or black.*
Photography by Patricia Canino

Geoffrey Scott

*M*ulti-disciplinary designer Geoffrey Scott of Venice, California, has been involved with projects involving architecture, interior design, furniture design and graphics for fifteen years. Addressing issues of ecology and longevity in an inventive, meaningless and timeless manner, he has extended his professional reach into the realms of research, publishing and teaching.

As a designer Scott has completed residential and commercial buildings and spaces for Saks Fifth Avenue, Nikon, Nations Bank, the LBJ Foundation, Meredith Brokaw and the University of Texas. As a researcher he has developed a furniture company, Materials for Living, and received grants from the American Institute of Architects and the Texas Society of Architects for work resulting in publications and for his thesis: "A New Urban Housing Type."

"Because my background is multi-disciplinary, I resist the temptation for my furniture to necessarily imitate my architecture. The scale and function of furniture is largely different from that of the building itself.

"Finnish architect Alvar Aalto understood this and responded sensitively by softening form and edges, and by using natural materials. Frank Lloyd Wright's furniture, on the other hand, was often a continuation of his thematic architecture, overemphasizing his genius for being able to manipulate a particular architectural vocabulary. The results too often are stiff and uncomfortable."

"The design of a piece is of paramount importance. The furniture I design must be well-conceived and pleasing in appearance inside and out. There is no such thing as a 'back,' 'inside' or 'underneath' which is unimportant. Each view should be stimulating, inventive, meaningful and timeless."

"The designer's responsibility is to individual clients and always to society as a whole. In the case of a private commission, the designer must understand the nature of the client—responding to the context, his or her needs, requirements and the uniqueness of the situation. Issues such as ergonomics and longevity should be resolved within this framework."

"To society, responsibility in furniture and all product design emphasizes ecology first. A society is profoundly influenced by design, for we in the profession have an opportunity to encourage the conservation of resources and the diminishment of pollution. Each piece of furniture should be designed and fabricated to last as long as appropriate for its function. Knockdown furniture, intended as disposable, should also be fully recyclable."

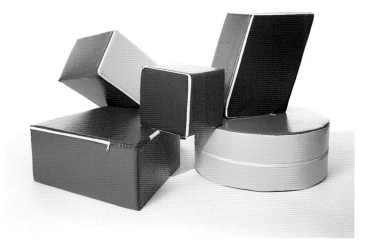

Soft Shapes for Kids/Materials for Living Interactive Table System. *Designed by Geoffrey Scott, 1987. Available through Geoffrey Scott Design Associates. Solicor exterior, wood structure. Photography by Hugo Rojas*

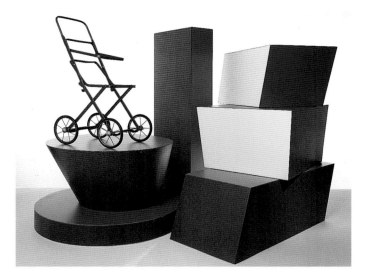

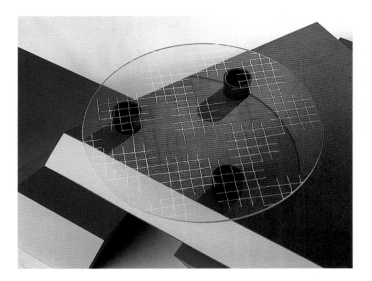

Shapes and Slabs/Materials for Living Interactive Table System. *Designed by Geoffrey Scott, 1987. Available through Geoffrey Scott Design Associates. Solicor exterior, wood structure. Optional table-top: silk-screened glass.*
Photography by Hugo Rojas

Ward Bennett

O ne of Amerca's seminal designers whose work spans more than five decades, Ward Bennett began his career as a fashion illustrator in New York City during the early 1930s. Studying design under Brancusi and Le Corbusier and painting under Hans Hoffman, Bennett initially pursued sculpture but decided, in 1947, on a career designing residential

interiors. Throughout his interior design work, Ward Bennett has espoused a minimalist philosophy which became the signature of contemporary interiors in the '60s and '70s. In addition to his long association with Brickel Associates designing seating, Bennett in 1991 created a new twenty-two-piece collection of furniture for Geiger International. His works are part of the permanent collections of the Museum of Modern Art and the Smithsonian's Cooper-Hewitt Museum, both in New York.

"I cannot separate architecture from interiors—they are one and the same thing for me. So designing buildings and interiors and furniture is the same."

"I cannot separate the design from its fabrication or its function. They are all very exciting, beautiful and creative."

"The responsibility of the designer? To produce a design that is functional and comfortable."

Triad Table. *Designed by Ward Bennett, 1990. Manufactured by Geiger International. Shown in the living area Mr. Bennett designed for his own home in East Hampton, Long Island, New York. One of seventeen designs, which form the basis of the collection's initial introduction and its hundreds of individual model variations. Each has been patented, and each carries Bennett's personal trademark on every model. Shown with a bust from Cambodia and candlesticks which Bennett uses as paperweights. Photography by Michael Mundy*

Paul Tuttle

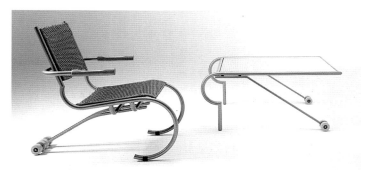

*P*aul Tuttle of Santa Barbara, California, is known almost as well for his irreverence for history and philosophy as he is for his remarkably fresh design. Perhaps, in his case, one led to the other.

Tuttle, who studied at Art Center College of Design and Frank Lloyd Wright's Taliesen West, has been associated with various architectural firms, but it is through his furniture design for manufacturers such as Strassle and Atelier International that most people have become familiar with his work. He has been much awarded by his peers throughout the past decade. One-man exhibitions of his designs have been held with regularity in both California and Switzerland where he spends many months every year living and creating.

"How does my being involved with architecture and interiors affect my perspective as a furniture designer? It doesn't. Furniture, for me, has to do almost strictly with the sensitivities of the human body...the touch...the eye...."

"For me, design and fabrication and function are all part of the whole. I don't think otherwise."

"The responsibility of the designer? I don't think I have an answer to this question."

The Skate Series/Table, shown with The Skate Series Lounge Chair. *Designed by Paul Tuttle, 1993. Manufactured by Strassle Sohne & Co. Represented in the U.S. by Atelier Interrnational, Ltd. Steel frame table with clear wire-glass or ceramic top which can be used indoors and outdoors. Steel frame is zinc-coated for corrosion resistance. Heat-fused polyester powder-coated gray finish. Chair can be ordered with synthetic rattan or nylon mesh, both UV treated and resistant to the sun's rays. Photography courtesy of Strassle Sohne & Co.*

Table. *Designed by Paul Tuttle, 1990. Crafted by Jeff Walker. Available through the designer. Metal, glass and marble. Photography by Assassi Productions*

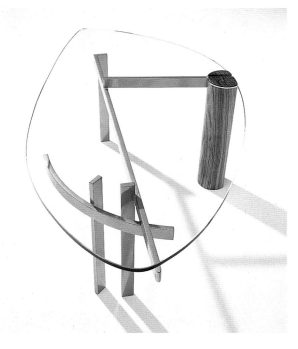

Coffee Table. *Designed by Paul Tuttle, 1992. Metal crafted by Jeff Walker. Available through the designer. Metal, glass and wood. Photography by Assassi Productions*

Robert A.M. Stern

*R*obert A.M. Stern is a practicing architect, teacher and writer. Founder and senior partner in the firm of Robert A.M. Stern Architects of New York, he is a Fellow of the American Institute of Architects and received the Medal of Honor from its New York Chapter in 1984.

A professor at the Graduate School of Architecture, Planning and Preservation at Columbia University and presently (1993) Director of the Historic Preservation Department, Stern served from 1984 to 1988 as the

first director of Columbia's Temple Hoyne Buell Center for the Study of American Architecture. He has lectured extensively in the United States and abroad on both historical and contemporary topics in architecture. He is the author of several books including *New Directions in American Architecture, George Howe: Toward a Modern American Architecture,* and *Modern Classicism.*

Stern is a graduate of Columbia University (Bachelor of Arts, 1960) and Yale University (Master of Architecture, 1965).

"To me, furniture is often architecture in miniature. I think this has always been true of the most interesting furniture. Philip Johnson's AT&T Building is not a blown-up Chippendale highboy; a Chippendale highboy is a reduced version of a building. I have designed furniture and tabletop items that resemble portions of a building pulled into the scheme of a room."

"Design and function are both of paramount importance. Fabrication, whether it involves lasers or traditional woodcarving—and my furniture has used each, is just the means for realizing the design: tools to be mastered by craftspeople whose work combined with that of the architect comprises the design process."

"Ergonomics is a pretentious word for comfort. A chair should suit the human proportion and the task—but a chair is not a body stocking. And whatever one does should be done as beautifully and as solidly as possible. Architecture and furniture, alike, should be forever...."

Dining Table and Sideboard.

Designed for a private residence by Robert

A.M. Stern. Dining table: rosewood,

satinwood, ebony. Sideboard: rosewood,

satinwood, ebony, granite. Fabricated by

Volz Clarke & Associates. Fleur-de-lis

marquetry by Silas Kopf.

John Chan

*A*s design director and founder of John Chan Design Ltd. in Hong Kong, John Chan is involved in the creation of the total ambience of a project—from interior planning and materials selection to restaurant and guest room graphics and the design of signage and uniforms.

Born in Hong Kong, Chan studied three-dimensional design at Berkshire College in England, majoring in interior and exhibition design, and stage design at City Lit, London. After returning to the Orient, he spent a year teaching interior and exhibition design at the Meng Chuien University in Taipei, later becoming involved in the design of projects such as the Taipei Regency Hotel, the Taipei Sheraton Hotel, the Caesar Park Hotel in Kenting, and the American Club in China, Taipei. From Taiwan, Chan returned to Hong Kong where from 1984 to 1990 he designed the Grand Hyatt Melbourne, Grand Hyatt in Hong Kong as well as Taipei for Hirsch/Bedner and Associates's Hong Kong office. His most recent projects include the Seibu Department Store in Hong Kong, Uraku Tower in Hawaii, Uraku Placeo in Aoyama, Tokyo, Sunrise Golf Club and Hotel in Taipei and the renovation of Lane Crawford Central Department Store in Hong Kong.

Apart from hotels and clubs, Chan has designed prestigious restaurants as well as some of Hong Kong's most talked about boutiques and salons. He is also actively involved in the theater world, designing stage sets, costumes and lighting. In 1991 he received the Stage Designer of the Year Award from the Hong Kong Artists Guild.

"I have always believed that interior design is a creation of a certain atmosphere and environment within a given structure. Everything inside is part of the whole act. Furniture as well as artifacts, lighting, graphics, staff uniforms—all are of equal importance. My furniture design is part of my interior design."

"The three—design, function and fabrication—go hand in hand. However, one could look at the space and decide whether a sculptural or a functional piece should be used to suit the mood."

"From the business point of view, function and cost effectiveness seem to be the designer's most important responsibilities.
"From the artistic point of view, reflection of the designer's individuality, character and innovation seem most important.
"From my own point of view, both of the above."

John Chan Collection. Designed by John Chan, 1991 and 1992. Side tables, coffee/tea table, dining table and desk. Distributed through Designer Imports Ltd., Hong Kong. The distinctive edge design was taken from an antique Japanese bow and arrow set which is represented in the collection by rosewood, walnut and sycamore veneer and ash burl or olive burl insets. Legs are either stained black ash or natural maple. Photography by Raymond Yui Chan

Peter Wooding

*P*eter Wooding is a multi-faceted designer working throughout a broad spectrum of design. He is well known as both an interior and an industrial designer. His career began more than twenty-five years ago at Herman Miller Research under Robert Propst in Ann Arbor, Michigan. Later he became the Design Director of the non-profit, multi-discipline Research and Design Institute (REDE). In 1978, he and his wife JoAnn opened Peter Wooding Design Associates headquartered in Providence, Rhode Island. Their practice today ranges from total facilities development to tabletop products.

"Being an interior designer gives me a broader view when designing furniture, in that I look at the whole context of environment and use. In my role as an industrial designer, I think about the user—his or her comfort, safety, enjoyment both physically and aesthetically. I also think about the material—how to bring out the best qualities of the wood, the leather....I also think of the manufacturing processes and procedures. How can it be made most efficiently, cost-effectively, time effectively. But, since I'm also an interior designer, I go further. I think about the furniture in its context of the room and how furniture is a vehicle to express personality, and how it helps to define space and relate to all that is around it."

"Any successful design is made up of three component parts: a good designer, a good builder or manufacturer, and a good client. Without any of the three component parts, the design will be lacking. No matter how great the design may be in the abstract, if it is not fabricated beautifully, or doesn't function as intended, it's not a great design. No matter how beautifully fabricated a poor design may be, it is still a poor design and no matter how attractive or well fabricated a piece or product may be, if it doesn't do an excellent job of fulfilling its function, it becomes sculpture or something else, but not a design of a great piece of furniture."

"I believe that the designer's responsibility is to create beautiful things that work. The designer must be an advocate for the end-user to create a piece of furniture that exceeds the user's expectations and, consequently, always delights. That includes all aspects of a product: its look, its feel, the way it functions, the way it improves with age, the knowledge that the materials were responsibly chosen. On our Portsmouth chair, for instance, there is an extra bonus. It's the feel of that curve on the inside of the spiral at the end of the arm. When you are sitting in the chair, your hands just naturally gravitate to that feature—it just feels great and it is at your fingertips in the natural course of sitting in the chair."

Belmont Conference/Dining Table and Portsmouth Armchairs. *Designed by Peter Wooding in 1993 and 1992 respectively. Manufactured by Gilbert International. Chairs available in mahogany, maple, cherry, walnut and high-gloss opaque polyresin diamond finish in thirty-six colors. Upholstery is custom or Gilbert Leather or Stratford Hall textiles. Shown is Donghia raffia weave. Table is available in maple (shown), or mahogany, cherry or walnut and in several sizes. Line includes occasional tables and a console table. Photography by Warren Jagger*

Margaret Helfand

*E*stablished in 1981, Margaret Helfand Architects has been engaged in a broad diversity of commercial, institutional and residential projects ranging from adaptive reuse to new construction. The firm's work has been published in national and international publications and has won numerous design awards.

The firm's architecture explores new approaches to generating form, organizing space and constructing architectural and interior elements. Specific functional and structural requirements are reduced to their basic components and then become the expressive language of each project. Stone, metal, glass, wood and simple structural systems are the common denominators of all projects. Forms, frequently irregular and unexpected, are gen-

erated by context, program requirements or method of construction. This highly rational approach to design, greatly influenced by the tenets of early twentieth-century Modernism, clearly seeks a new sense of order from within the process of design and construction itself rather than relying on the traditional sources of historic forms or preconceived theoretical constructs.

Helfand has lectured on her firm's work at the American Craft Museum in connection with its recent Architectural Art exhibition, at SCI-ARC, the Southern California Institute of Architecture, and at Columbia University. She also serves frequently as guest critic at the graduate schools of architecture at Columbia University, Yale University, University of Pennsylvania and Pratt Institute.

"Architecture and furniture represent two ends of a continuum of design to solve human needs. We conceive of each in exactly the same terms and investigate solutions with exactly the same process. Vitruvius had it right when he described architecture as the integration of 'firmness, commodity and delight.' We follow this mandate in celebrating structure, purpose and art as the genesis of each design project."

"We cannot imagine design without its being rooted in function or fabrication. These are what design is all about!"

"We accept our responsibility to create simple, elegant and timeless solutions which reflect rigorous internal logic and are appropriate to their context."

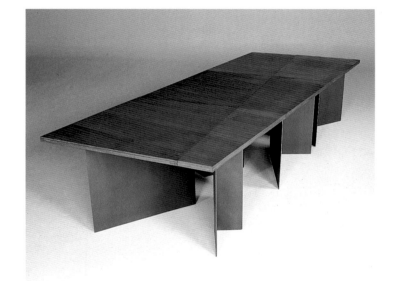

Table in Six Segments. *Designed by Margaret Helfand Architects, ©1992. Bases: ¼ inch folded steel plate, garnet blasted, satin polyurethane finish. Tops: 1½ inch multi-ply with maple veneer, clear lacquer with bronze dust finish.*

Samuel Botero

"*I* like a mixture of periods and styles, and in the case of the Pyramid Collection, which was introduced in 1992, I was inspired to interpret the Egyptian vocabulary of shapes, such as obelisks and the pyramids," says Colombian-born Samuel Botero who early in his career developed a continuing clientele who have been drawn to the vigor, as well as the refinement, of his creative approach.

Botero, who attended Pratt Institute, was associated with a number of architectural and interior design firms before founding Samuel Botero Associates, Inc. in New York City in 1980.

"Being an interior designer, I have learned how people live. Through this knowledge I have become aware of the needs and requirements that should be met in good furniture design."

"Function, design and fabrication are all important in furniture design. First is the thought process to determine the function, which in turn leads to the design. Second is the aesthetic or the design itself. Third comes the fabrication, how each piece is to be executed, which can make or break a good design."

"The responsibility of a designer is to give people a product that has the best possible value, is of excellent quality, and is made of materials that are responsible to the environment."

Desk, from the Pyramid Collection. Designed by Samuel Botero, 1992. Lace wood, ebony and leather. Various colors and finishes. Collection includes case-goods, seating, and desks. Available through the designer.
Photography by Robert Bardel/Visions

Leavitt/Weaver   Craig Leavitt ◦ Stephen Weaver

*T*he style of Craig Leavitt and Stephen Weaver, who founded their firm in 1976 in California's San Joaquin Valley, might be cavalierly classified as modern. However its non-static intuitive design gestures often draw from a variety of international and historical influences...as well

as from a huge dose of self-imposed whimsy.

Leavitt/Weaver offers an entire line of furniture and accessories to the trade through Randolph and Hein showrooms in San Francisco, Los Angeles and New York and in the Chicago region through Holly Hunt Limited. The firm's recent interior design commissions include Plump Jack Cafe and Wine Shop, San Francisco; Northwest Airlines, Tokyo; and Geoffrey Beene, New York.

"Being involved with the entire realm of interior design enables us to know what's missing in the marketplace. It also encourages us to design pieces that work within the context of the entire project."

"It's all right for furniture design to be deadly serious, but nothing need die in the process."

"Our decorating is often influenced by 'found' materials and objets d'art."

Squiggle Side Table. *Designed by Leavitt/Weaver, 1990. Aluminum and steel. Finish shown: ivory, nickel and jade.*
Photography by James K. Fanning

Modern Console. *Designed by Leavitt/Weaver, 1989. Steel and aluminum. Finish shown: faux bois and bronze.*
Photography by James K. Fanning

Spiral Table. *Designed by*
Leavitt/Weaver, 1992. Steel.
Finish shown: brushed steel.
Photography by James K. Fanning

Elyse B. Lacher

*E*lyse Lacher is president of Cy Mann International, a firm she co-founded with her father, Emanuel Lacher, over twenty-six years ago as a subsidiary of an existing corporation. Under her direction, the company has achieved a position in the interior furnishings industry as a major supplier of high-end contemporary furniture to both commercial and residential markets. Lacher not only has established a national network of showroom distribution but also is personally responsible for development of the firm's ever-expanding collection. She herself designs almost 60 percent of the pieces; the remainder is selected and styled by her from sources discovered during years of travel.

A graduate of Queens College with a Bachelor's degree in Speech Pathology, she has an educational background in design from Pratt Institute and the New York School of Interior Design.

"As an interior designer, you are more aware of the day-to-day problems that must be addressed before designing the actual interior space. Not only must you consider size, shape and proportion of a room but also you must take into account the needs of your client for function, practicality and comfort.

"Contemporary products are what is happening now! It is an asset to have the ability to draw from my experience as an interior designer when developing furniture products. For example, it definitely influences my decisions with regard to scale, function and choice of materials."

"Sometimes the idea for a design comes from a need for a product; other times an introduction or a new material stimulates the need for a new design. I believe, other than an accessory item, the design and function are interrelated. They come first. The proper fabrication becomes important when executing the first two successfully."

"It is my opinion that 'ergonomics' is an extremely important concept when dealing with the level of comfort required for good seating today, whether it be a residential or contract product. A designer should be well versed in the latest technologies available to be incorporated within his or her designs, whether it be lower lumbar supports or different densities of foam. At the same time, we must keep in mind the new manufacturing techniques available with regard to preserving our ecology. You cannot design in a vacuum and be successful."

The Jewel Collection. *Designed by Elyse Lacher, 1987. Manufactured by Cy Mann International. Coffee tables: brass or stainless steel with inset metal details, with various pigmentations from a metallurgical dye process that renders the coloration integral to the material. Six colors—emerald, sapphire, gold, topaz, ruby and onyx—are offered in a choice of brushed or mirrored finish. The names of the five individual bases— Solitaire, Marquise, Emerald, Cabochon and Baguette—further the tables' association with fine jewels. Various configurations, sizes, and stone tops available. Photography by Mark Ross*

Solitaire

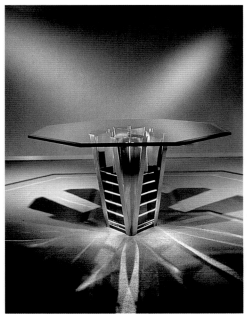

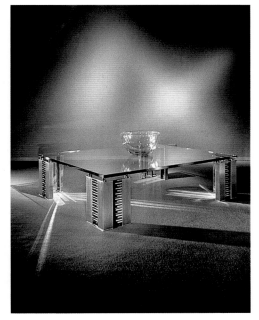

Marquise

Emerald

Oscar Tusquets Blanca

Architect by formation, painter by inclination and designer by vocation, Oscar Tusquets Blanca is the prototype of the integral artist who has been progressively condemned to extinction by the specialization of the modern world. Nonetheless, his work today is part of the collection of several museums around the world: Centre Georges Pompidou in Paris, the Metropolitan Museum of Art, Avery Library at Columbia University and the Museum of Modern Art in New York, The Israel Museum of Jerusalem, Teatre Museu Dali in Figueras, Musée des Arts Decoratifs in Paris, Vitra Design Museum in Germany, Architektur Museum in Frankfurt, Die Neue Sammlung de Munich, and Deutsches Klingenmuseum in Solingen.

Born in 1941 in Barcelona, his first steps in the artistic discipline were at the Escuela de Artes y Oficios and at the Escuela Superior de Arquitectura de Barcelona, from which he graduated in 1965. He co-founded Studio Per, dissolved since 1984, and the B.D. Ediciones de Diseño, a production company for which he began his designs of furniture and objects. His relation with Italian design companies has become increasingly close over the years and has extended to prestigious industrialists in Spain and other countries. In 1987, with Carlos Diaz, he founded the professional firm Tusquets, Diaz & Associates for the development of his architectural work as a whole.

"Certainly, being an architect helps me greatly in furniture design, especially to detect some problems for which it is difficult to find a solution in the market. My designs seldom derive from a specific technology or material. Rather they come from a situation for which I cannot find the furniture I like."

"The design cannot disassociate itself from function. We love an object when we use it in an easy and sensual way. We end up hating it when it is full of difficulties or problems. In my opinion, it is absolutely reductive to limit the aesthetics of one object to the field of vision (and even sometimes to the photogenic field) without considering the tactile, auditive, or thermatic field, among others."

"The responsibility of a designer is the same as any other artist, to be innovative and at the same time understood."

Girandola. *Designed by Oscar Tusquets Blanca, 1993. Produced by Carlos Jané Camacho, 1993. A medium-size table which can be unfolded. Its leaves can be brought up gracefully, according to the designer, "to save anti-aesthetic gymnastic exercises."*

"If the coffee table in the sitting room is small," says Tusquets, "we have to make a real effort to reach the table from the sofa. If, on the other hand, it is too big, we cannot even pass by if there is someone sitting there."

Photography courtesy of Carlos Jané Camacho

Carlos and Gerard Pascal .

*B*rothers Carlos and Gerard Pascal of Mexico City cannot remember a time when furniture design was not a part of their practice. "Being architects and interior designers makes us see design as a whole," says Gerard. "Furniture design comes as a result of the same process, when the job we are doing asks itself for a specific design. It is just a matter of continuity."

Many times, he says, they select pieces that are already offered in the market. Yet many times, because of their being so involved with the architecture and interiors of a specific project, it is consequential that they should design certain pieces that serve as links to the total environment.

"Usually, when we don't find what we are looking for in the showrooms, we look in our minds," says Carlos. "Then, the dialogue begins, and the excitement of following the process until we see the finished product, its behavior as a functional piece, and, hopefully, its beauty."

"We behave as furniture designers the same way we do as architects or interior designers. There is order involved in the design process. We just follow it based on our experience and intuition, with an exploratory approach."

"The design, fabrication and function of a piece of furniture have the same importance...but at different times in the creative process. First comes function. Before we start designing we have to know what the piece will be, how it will be used, what size and proportions will be best for its function. Then we focus on style and the materials required for its fabrication. We experiment with traditional materials, trying to give them a new meaning. We also base our design on classical styles, giving them a fresh look, a new meaning."

"Our responsibility lies in creating something beautiful that works, that stimulates, and that gives pleasure to the senses aesthetically and functionally. That also means the design will be ruled by the aesthetics of the period to which it belongs. Yet the real value should be in its concept, so that it goes beyond trends and fashion and remains timeless. Intuition, memories and experience give to the design a sense of 'territorial identity,' meaning that even a new contemporary or unusual design could be referred to a classical order, giving the design a human and familiar scale."

Basamento Dining Table. *Designed by Carlos and Gerard Pascal, 1991. Columns of black stained ash wood, base of stainless steel with a patina with the appearance of light brass. Glass top. Manufactured by Brueton. Photography by Eitan Feinholz*

Canica Dining Table. *Designed by Carlos and Gerard Pascal, 1992. Sapele wood, stainless steel and glass balls. Manufactured by Brueton. Photography by Eitan Feinholz*

Angular Pedestal. *Designed by Carlos and Gerard Pascal, 1991. Steel and brushed brass. Manufactured by Studio Steel.*
Photography by Eitan Feinholz.

Columnata Dining Table. *Designed by Carlos and Gerard Pascal, 1990. Steel, brushed brass and granite, with a glass top. Manufactured by Studio Steel.*
Photography by Eitan Feinholz

Joseph Alcasar Terrell

*J*oseph Alcasar Terrell, curatorial specialist and founder/director of Alcasar Terrell, Inc., has made inroads into the residential and commercial design business by incorporating a curator's sensibility into the selection and space planning of art and furnishings. The Los Angeles based environmental designer has spent the last two decades working in the areas of design and fine arts for cultural institutions, commercial establishments and residential environments on both coasts.

PHOTOGRAPHY BY DAVID WILLIAMS

The Del Rey Colony Townhouse project in Venice, California, is an example of Terrell's combination of fine design with curatorial expertise. Completed in 1986, it won numerous design, marketing and architectural awards including "Project of the Year" from *Builder's* magazine.

Terrell, president of the board of trustees of the Millicent Rogers Museum in Taos, New Mexico, and board member/artistic director for Barnsdall Park and Municipal Arts Gallery Association in Los Angeles, says: "I am preoccupied with installations that are timelessly tasteful, spaces that support contemporary and historic art."

"As a designer, I suspect that I'm normally influenced and affected by those in my profession who have made landmark contributions in our field ...Corbu, Mies, the Bauhaus boys and girls, Stickley, Green and Green. Coupled with this appreciation is an undying attraction to primitive, folk and historic art and furniture. These elements provide me with the tools from which I can create and design furniture, and I occasionally use them when I can't find what I need in the marketplace."

"Design and form, I'm afraid to admit, are my priority. Other aspects of furniture are important, but not as...."

"I'm incapable of contemplating design on a short-term basis. Timeless environments and designs are what I'm influenced by, and therefore what I try to produce. If I'm successful, they somehow give me integrity and perhaps longevity...."

Hippo Table. *Designed by Joseph Terrell and Charles Greer, 1990. Available through Alcasar Terrell, Inc. Sandblasted glass, industrial bolts and screws, oiled steel or powder-coated-white pencil shaped legs. Photography by Grey Crawford*

Amerasian Table. Designed by Joseph
Terrell and Ken Matazonni, 1992.
Fabricated by Creative Woodworks.
Available through Alcasar Terrell, Inc.
Maple, safety plate glass. Accompanied
by dove-tailed-mitered chairs.
Photography by Grey Crawford

Antonio Citterio

*A*ntonio Citterio was born in Meda in 1950 and graduated from the Polytechnic in Milan with a degree in architecture and immediately pursued work in architecture and design. Since 1972 he has worked primarily in the field of industrial design as a designer and consultant, and with many furniture manufacturers including B&B Italia and Vitra.

Among his many prestigious commissions are the Esprit headquarters in Milan and Amsterdam. In 1986 Terry Dwan became a partner in the firm, which was renamed Studio Citterio Dwan. They were then given the commission for a third Esprit headquarters in Antwerp as well as the store's

fixturing system for Europe. In 1992 Citterio built the Polsterfabrik in Neuenburg for Vitra and completetd an industrial complex in Milan for Antonio Fusco. In Japan, in partnership with Toshiyuki Kita, the firm completed the headquarters in Kobe for World Company and recently the Corrente Building in Tokyo.

Citterio has taught at Domus Academy in Milan and has participated in many exhibitions, including independent shows in Hanover, Rome, Amsterdam, Paris and Weil. In 1992 he was responsible for the original concept and layout of the exhibition "Objets et Projets" in Paris, and took part in an invited competition for hospital ward furniture organized by the French Ministry of Culture.

"My work as both architect and designer at the same time has given me a wider experience of projects in all scales. Duality is the 'fil rouge' which characterizes my daily work. It allows an exchange of ideas between the design and the architectural fields."

"The designed object can be separated neither from its method of production nor from its function. I always pay great attention to technical innovation, but the end product does not need to show this. More importantly, it has to be a rediscovery of the emotional value that goes beyond the mere matching of form and function."

"A very recent aspect of our work is to draw attention to the phases of the lifespan of materials in their environmental context. Bearing recycling in mind, I am trying to distance my products from the realm of the 'overdesigned'; I am convinced that the best results are obtained by understatement."

Battista. *Designed by Antonio Citterio with Oliver Löw, 1992. Manufactured by Kartell s.p.a. Folding extension table with a large top which can be used as a single table, a service table or a buffet cart. Accordion-like design permits a partial or total folding of the top. Top: structural rigid polyurethane with scratch-proof finishing. Frame: chromium-plated steel. Foot: polished aluminum. Colors: black, sea-blue, curry, fir, plum.*
Photography by Miro Zagnoli

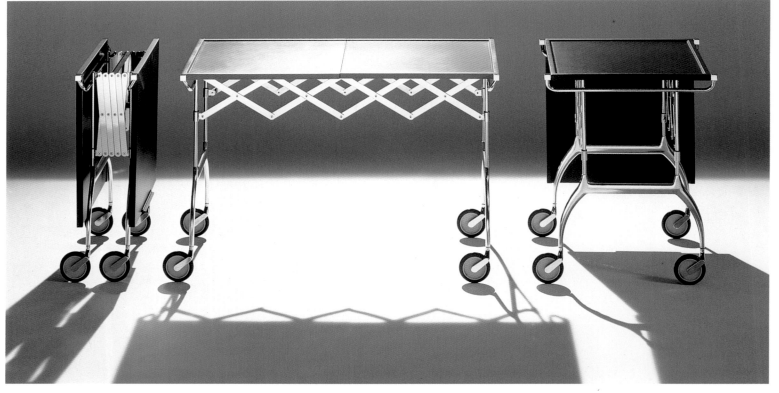

Bradley Rath

*C*hicago furniture designer Bradley Rath has been on the leading edge of studio design furniture in metal since the mid-1980s. He is well known and respected in the design industry and is the founder and president of the Chicago Furniture Designers Association, CFDA—a not-for-profit association dedicated to the promotion and advancement of Chicago furniture art.

After graduating with a Bachelor of Fine Arts degree from Roosevelt University in Chicago, Rath began his furniture design career at the Karl Mann showroom in 1987. Two years later, he opened his own studio in Chicago where he designed, manufactured and produced his own work. Presently his work is manufactured and produced at his atelier in Madison, Wisconsin, although his permanent residence is in Chicago.

Rath has designed various public use installations and interiors for restaurants, cafes, night clubs, galleries and boutiques.

"My perspective is rather different than one might expect. I began in the design field as a furniture designer, which is still my greatest passion. I began to get requests from my furniture clients to space plan and design different aspects of their environments. It was both challenging and rewarding to be able to design a space that enhanced the impact of my furniture. I believe that this has made me a better designer overall. I discovered that I could express myself more completely by taking more into consideration than just the furniture."

"The overall design is the most important. This includes the considerations of fabrication and the furniture's function as well. My belief is that, for a spectacular finale, all things should be considered as one. I cannot produce a design without paying attention to each aspect and detail of the piece. I have a fabrication background, therefore engineering is almost second nature, which I feel gives me a real advantage to be able to produce a timeless, functional high quality piece of furniture."

"I like to think of my furniture design as being timeless in appearance, and my spinning spheres—for the spherical motifs in these tables do spin—are a symbol of the growing importance of global awareness and ecology."

Bar Table, End Table, Console Table and Dining Table. *Designed by Bradley Rath, 1993. Recycled Type 304 stainless steel, granite and, in the dining table, glass. Shown with bar stools also designed by Bradley Rath. Available through Betty M Showroom, Chicago. Photography courtesy of Integra Communications, Chicago*

Sherle Wagner

*S*herle Wagner has brought his knowledge of architecture and love of classical design and sculpture to the creation of "works of art that work." As president of Sherle Wagner International, the firm Wagner and his wife started more than forty-seven years ago, he pioneered the concept of the luxury bathroom.

Wagner chose his path apart from the assembly line and tumult of the traditional marketplace. He opted for the unique and luxe in materials, a strong sculptural influence in design, and was the first to introduce the finest of onyx and semi-precious stone into the bath environment. It was the natural beauty and rare colorings of these semi-precious stones that became the inspiration behind the debut of his "limited edition" collection of opulently proportioned, yet streamlined in design, tables.

"Although I attended architectural school, it is an inherent appreciation of art and sculpture that has been enormously inspiring and an overriding design influence. My knowledge of architecture, along with a love of classical design, brings everything into a singular focus. One can create for oneself on a personal basis, but when one creates for the architectural and design industries, business criteria as well as aesthetic requirements must be considered."

"Design, fabrication and function are all very important to me. There is no question about the importance of aesthetics, the balance, the line, the medium, and so forth. Yet a piece must always function superbly in its intended environment and for its intended purpose. Of course, quality is paramount. Not only should a product be beautifully crafted and gracefully conceived but also it should be built to last a very long time."

"Every human being must take a share of the responsibility for the preservation of the world's ecological balance. A designer has a special obligation to work with materials that uphold this commitment. We deal largely in natural materials that are mineral based. We incorporate nothing that is endangered and we do not use skins of any kind. If the product has overall design integrity and quality, it will allow the client to create a distinctive, consistently designed living environment that will sustain for many years."

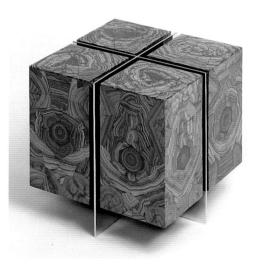

Cube Table. *Designed by Sherle Wagner, 1985. Manufactured through Sherle Wagner International. Malachite and stainless steel.*
Photography courtesy of Sherle Wagner International

Coffee Table. *Designed by Sherle Wagner, 1985. Manufactured through Sherle Wagner International. Malachite with faceted steel corners, each accented with a triangular insert of the malachite.*
Photography courtesy of Sherle Wagner International

Mark Simon

Mark Simon is one of five partners at Centerbrook Architects and Planners in Essex, Connecticut, a firm with twenty·eight years experience in architecture and planning, a staff of fifty-six, and a national practice.

The son of sculptor Sidney Simon, he learned about wood and design at an early age, developing his own sculptural skills and later studying under Peter Grippe, Michael Mazur and Nicholas Carone at Brandeis where he

received a Bachelor of Arts degree, graduating cum laude with honors in sculpture in 1968. After receiving a Master's Degree in Architecture from Yale University, he initially worked as a cabinetmaker; later in the office of Warren Platner he learned a concern for architectural detail. Moving to work with Charles Moore, his former teacher, in 1974, he collaborated on a

series of houses. He became a partner in Moore Grover Harper, now Centerbrook, in 1978, soon receiving awards for his work which had broadened to include commercial and institutional projects. In 1990 he was advanced to the American Institute of Architects College of Fellows.

Simon has taught architectural design at Yale, Harvard, University of Maryland, Carnegie Mellon, and North Carolina State University. Among his recent commissions as project architect is the $50 million Nauticus, the National Maritime Center in Norfolk, Virginia, an ambitious interactive museum attraction on the downtown waterfront.

"I think about how furniture defines space."

"I consider the structures of furniture, the shape of furniture, and the choreography of people using furniture."

"The design often evolves from thoughts about function and fabrication. They are all necessarily intertwined. I keep designing until all three are happily satisfied."

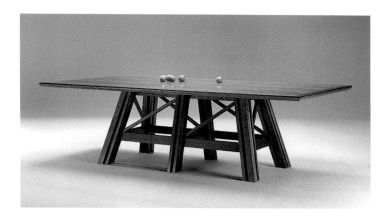

Simon Group Tables. *Designed by Mark Simon, 1990. Manufactured by Gilbert International. Mahogany, cherry or maple. Available in two sizes as a dining/conference table or as a smaller coffee table with a glass top. Winner of the 1993 Honor Award of the Institute of Business Designers.*

Bobby Cadwallader, former president of Knoll and now consultant for Gilbert International, saw a photograph of a dining table Simon had designed for a private home and asked him to adapt that table for commercial use and mass-production. Reminiscent of many things...old artists' easels, modern bridge framing, early American rustic furniture...it seems equally comfortable in a corporate or residential setting.

Photography by Tom Helmick/Gilbert International, Inc.

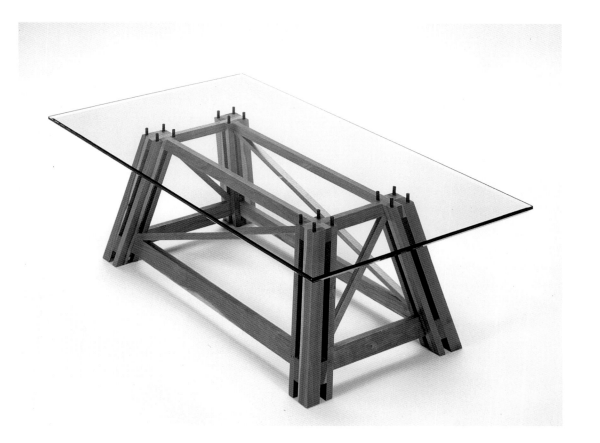

Eric Owen Moss

*E*ric Owen Moss, FAIA, sees furniture design as he does architecture —"as a new opportunity in making: a new method, a new tool or machine, a different material."

As in his buildings, in his furniture Moss deals in unpretentious materials, or materials which in another setting may have a different definition. For example, what was once known as a door in his work may be a table. His focus always is on the craft and in its clarity and dexterity. Also, as in the buildings he has designed, his furniture consistently refers to technology. "The model for furniture is the ubiquitous machine," he says, "a hybrid view of the machine as omnipresent, not as an idol or as an ideal, but with conflicting aspects both positive and negative."

Since Eric Owen Moss Architects was established in Culver City, California, in 1974, it has completed a broad range of public, corporate and hospitality spaces as well as private residences and has received a number of significant design awards. Moss, the architect for every project, works with a team of twenty professionals and provides, in addition to architectural and interior design services, considerable expertise in planning and programming studies.

Kitchen, Coffee and Dining Tables.
Designed by Eric Owen Moss for the Lawson/Westen House, Culver City, California, 1992. Bent plywood with mahogany veneer and acrylic tops, rubber rollerskate stops. Metal work and acrylic drilling by Tom Farrage and Company. Woodwork and bent plywood by Max Borghese.
Photography by Paul H. Groh

"At some level, every project involves a kind of manipulation or transformation of what's given either literally or figuratively, or both. What I don't want to do is give you back something that is monochromatic, single-minded (somehow single-minded and simple-minded are close to each other) so that if something is simply symmetrical, or simply balanced, or simply linear, or simply a narrative, then it's simple-minded. My experience of the world is not that."

"There's a hedonism here (love of joinery, love of assembly, love of the artifact) not in a repetitive, 'off the shelf' way, but more introverted and personal."

"The point is that to get these things done, and out, requires a kind of interrelationship with the world where you have to pass yourself off as a participant in that discussion.

"And that means redefining real and unreal with reference to the 'hardheaded' version of reality. Does the bank define what's real, or are you prepared to contest that? When you contest it, you're attacked, as though you're oblivious, or simple-minded, or some sort of knucklehead—as though you don't really know how the world works. And how does the world really work? That changes, too. I'm prepared to say I can alter that perception, even if it's an exception. It can be done. Not only in your head, but out there. And people will recognize it. I think that's the objective."

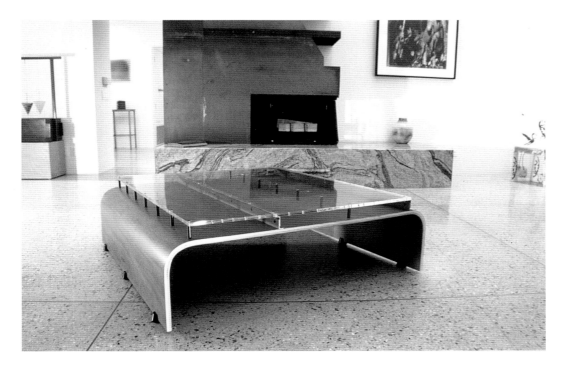

Sally Sirkin Lewis

*I*n 1972, interior designer Sally Sirkin Lewis and her husband Bernard Lewis opened the firm J. Robert Scott & Associates in Los Angeles, featuring her own line of furniture and textiles as well as representing many other leading U.S. home furnishings manufacturers. J. Robert Scott is represented nationally in all major cities as well as operates its own showrooms

in Los Angeles and Laguna Niguel, and New York City. Lewis herself continues to maintain a small interior design staff for a limited number of international and domestic clients. In addition to the many U.S. government design patents she has received for product designs, she has been the recipient of numerous design awards and was inducted into the Interior Design Hall of Fame in 1989.

"Being an interior designer affords me the opportunity of understanding people's needs and lifestyles. Consequently, I am hopefully able to translate these factors into my designs for furnishings and textiles."

"Good design is the sum of all its parts. It must be visually aesthetic and produced with quality, as well as fulfill practical requirements of the end user."

"The designer today needs to incorporate those materials and manners of production which will not further endanger our planet. Furthermore, our designs should stand the tests of time both aesthetically and practically, and, above all, our designs should conform to the ongoing and changing needs of our society."

Empire Hall Table. *Designed by Sally Sirkin Lewis, 1992. Hand applied macassar ebony wood veneer in a sunburst pattern on top. Hand carved heads and feet on alder wood legs. Chamfered apron and hand carved edge molding. Hand rubbed high polish lacquer finish with twenty-two-carat water gilded heads and feet and hand painted faux ivory filet. Companion design available: Empire Side Table. Manufactured by J. Robert Scott & Associates, Inc. Photography courtesy of J. Robert Scott & Associates, Inc.*

Snail Console. *Designed by Sally Sirkin Lewis, 1990. U.S. Patent #DES 325, 484. Hand carved snails and beading in alder wood with calfskin leather wrapped inset top. Hand applied and highly burnished water gilded silver leaf finish with contrasting bronze glaze. Manufactured by J. Robert Scott & Associates, Inc. Photography courtesy of J. Robert Scott & Associates, Inc.*

Marquetry III Tea Table. *Designed by Sally Sirkin Lewis, 1992. Design patent pending. Hand applied korina wood veneer top with sunburst pattern. Scalloped border, apron and saber legs in high polished black lacquer. Macassar ebony wood veneer inlay with aniline dyed stripe border. Hand rubbed high polish lacquer finish. Manufactured by J. Robert Scott & Associates, Inc. Photography courtesy of J. Robert Scott & Associates, Inc.*

Exxus Table. *Designed by Sally Sirkin Lewis, 1990. U.S. Design Patent #DES 332, 361. Metal clad X-shaped base connected by solid metal spheres. Brushed stainless steel with satin light bronze detailing. Bronze glass top with flat polished edges. Manufactured by J. Robert Scott & Associates, Inc. Photography courtesy of J. Robert Scott & Associates, Inc.*

CHAIRS

Dennis Jenkins

Lisa Bottom

Charles W. Moore

Heather Faulding

Dhana Solish

Scott Johnson

Christian Astuguevieille

Kipp Stewart

Lenny Steinberg

Anna Castelli Ferrieri

Tao Ho

Juhani Pallasmaa

Frank O. Gehry

Thomas A. Heinz

Antti Nurmesniemi

Javier Mariscal

Kisho Kurokawa

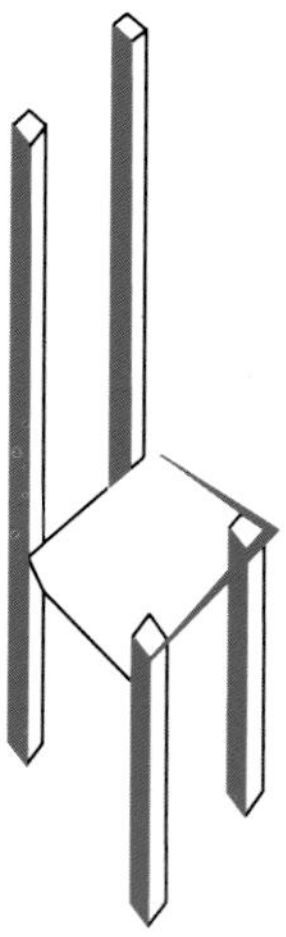

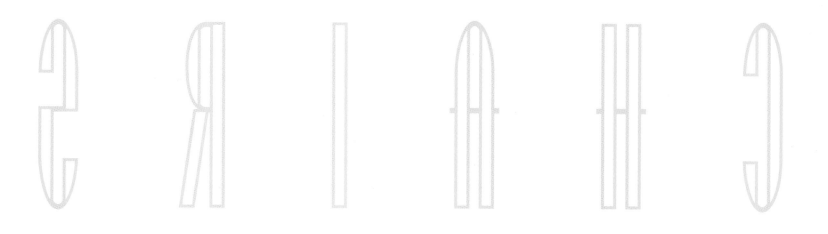

Mario Botta

Yrjö Kukkapuro

Mark Singer

Thayer Hopkins

Warren Snodgrass

Otto Zapf

Paul Haigh

Janice Feldman

Norman Sukkar

Warren Platner

Timothy deFiebre

Stan Taylor

Goralnick ★ Buchanan

José Luis Pérez Ortega

Mark Brazier-Jones

Nanna Ditzel

Dennis Jenkins

*I*nterior designer Dennis Jenkins of South Miami, Florida, says the main difference between his work process and that of an architect is that he is working from the inside out as opposed to having to provide the primary shelter. "I have been concerned with creativity through reflection of the individual client's personality and etching those concepts into the work by crafting my interiors," he says. "Having said that and having been in my field for thirty years, I have reached a position where I am totally enthralled with virtually all facets of the field of interiors and styles of furnishings. I enjoy grappling with all periods of history and designs from all over the world.

"However, I would personally feel incomplete and dissatisfied if I did not attempt to create 'the new.' I love working on that edge. I love being in the metal shop, the cabinet shop, millwork shop or the upholstery shop

observing and participating in making. It is an insatiable feeling, being totally immersed in creation, working on a piece that is reaching so far out there, so to the edge, that anxiety persists. But when successful, one is rewarded with a deep feeling of triumph. Moving society, getting the word out, all of this, means more to me than monetary gain. I have found that I need to create objects that evoke an emotional response and provoke a discussion. I would like to think that my work would be so striking, whether sublime or outlandish, that no one could pass it by without making comment."

Jenkins graduated from San Jose State College in 1964 and established Dennis Jenkins Design the next year. Since that time he has been involved in virtually all areas and scales of interior planning and design, including the design of custom and distinctive pieces of furniture.

"In terms of furniture design, for me, the concept 'working on the edge' reigns supreme. Function or the capacity of the piece to function as designed, fulfilling all the requirements of the proposed usage, follows. Fabrication is terribly important simply because a poorly constructed piece does not do justice to the integrity of the design concept and the subsequent required functions."

"Regarding the designer's responsibility, ergonomics, ecology and longevity are of varied value depending on the particular project specifics. It seems obvious that a seating piece should be comfortable and reflect a concern for the health of the individual user. Ecologically I am deeply concerned about the environment and am proud to be in the group called 'Green'...and there are always alternatives and sound solutions in the search for products that fulfill the needs of my furniture designs. Longevity as a concept is something that on the surface is positive, but if the product has no more useful life left, I say 'pull the plug' and get on with the new work."

Jester Barstool. *Designed by Dennis Jenkins, 1993. Steel. Fabricated by Stabil Indigo, Miami. Gold, silver and copper leaf applied by Ellen Moss. Photography by Dan Forer.*

Lounge Chair and Two Seater.

Designed by Dennis Jenkins, 1993. Steel
Fabricated by Stabil Indigo, Miami.
Photography by Dan Forer

Lisa Bottom

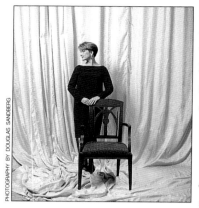

PHOTOGRAPHY BY DOUGLAS SANDBERG

*L*isa Bottom, principal for Bottom Duvivier of Redwood City, California, has more than fourteen years experience designing furniture showrooms and interiors for financial institutions, law offices, corporate offices and computer firms. She also is a product designer with several furniture lines currently being produced by large United States furniture manufacturers. Both aspects of her practice are evident in everything she does, she says.

"Certainly the experience I have had as an interior designer working on commercial projects has exerted a strong influence on developing durable designs. It also enabled me to see for myself just what was missing in the marketplace. I found a dearth of commercial pieces that had a special warmth and elegance that is often associated with antiques or one-of-a-kind items.

"What I also discovered in my years of practicing alongside other designers like myself was that most designers like to personalize a design but don't often have the budget or schedule to fabricate a truly custom design. As a result, almost all of my designs have the ability to be customized in one way or another, without becoming a special order product.

"The best example of this would be the Andras Dining Series, manufactured by HBF. This chair's appearance can be completely customized by the individual designer."

"To me, 'design' is a process of clearly defining a problem and taking steps toward creating a solution. As such, function and design are inseparable. The solution to the problem must be functional, or the object created becomes a styling exercise, and nothing more.

"Styling, or the act of creating an aesthetic statement, is a part of the design process. It is the look and feel of the object created, and because these things are the most immediately apparent, they are very important. However, the object must also be one that meets the needs of the user. One user need that has become increasingly important is to keep the cost of the items under control. To that end, fabrication is significant. If the style and structural integrity remains intact, but it is less expensive to fabricate the object one way versus another, the less expensive solution will better serve the needs of the user."

*"The responsibility of the designer is to **listen** to the needs of the end user, then translate these needs into something that is aesthetically pleasing and functional. Ergonomic issues are among the most basic functional issues, and, as such, are of course important. In addition, today environmental issues cannot be ignored. Creating beautiful things for posterity is meaningless if designers contribute to the destruction of the natural environment in the process."*

Andras Chair Series. *Designed by Lisa Bottom, 1990. Manufactured by HBF. Frame: carved from cherry. Seat upholstery available in both HBF fabrics or customer's own material. Offered as an alternative in both style and price to the more traditional Chippendale and Queen Anne dining chairs, this series is transitional in nature, incorporating some historical detailing with clean, elegant lines and form. The name Andras, derived from the Swedish verb "to change," identifies the series' chameleon-like nature. This collection is highly adaptable to the designer/specifier's needs, for the end product can be customized by using standard components. Building on a single frame, one can combine the options of six back panel inserts, three top rails and three arms or armless to create seventy-two alternative combinations. Photography by Herrington Olsen, Inc.*

Charles W. Moore

PHOTOGRAPHY BY NANCY WHITWORTH

*T*he late Charles W. Moore, FAIA, was an internationally acclaimed architect for more than four decades. He received the 1991 American Institute of Architects Gold Medal, the highest accolade given by the AIA, in "recognition of decades of an unfailing pursuit of design excellence, education, and professionalism." His work, writing and teaching have profoundly influenced the course of American architecture since his early award-winning work at Sea Ranch in Northern California in 1962.

Charles W. Moore Studio, in Austin, was established in 1984. In 1991 Moore and Arthur W. Andersson, his associate for seven years, formed Moore/Andersson Architects.

"Being an architect, I simply have an enthusiasm for designing objects and furniture, and in making things that might bring some sense of wonder or enjoyment to its owner."

"All three of these aspects—design, its fabrication and its function—are important, although I tend to focus these days more on the design of an object rather than its fabrication."

"My furniture tends to be very simple and in many ways ordinary, so I don't think that issues of ecology and longevity come into the picture. For instance, my Adirondack chair is mostly centered on being comfortable (which I guess is ergonomics) and through its proportions (extra wide armrests for iced tea) and color imparting a sense of delight."

The Adirondack Chair. *Designed by Charles W. Moore, 1993. Built of redwood and painted by Brian Wilgus. A limited production, numbered series. Available through Garden Follies, Austin.*

The Adirondack Chair is shown in Charles Moore's residence, keeping company with two Piranesi etchings and Charles Eames' bent plywood chair. Photography by Timothy Hursley

Heather Faulding

*S*outh African-born architect Heather Faulding always has emphasized conservation in her design, incorporating the new with the old and recycling existing materials and structure. Therefore, it was less a surprise than a joyful event when in 1993 Faulding Associates, now headquartered in New York, launched her Environmental Group including indoor/outdoor chairs that combine hand-beaten steel, Park Avenue poise, and childlike whimsy.

The chairs spring from a child's perception of trees and plants, conjuring up memories of early life in her native country, says Faulding. They are a little flip, she admits, but she was after a lighthearted approach to the increasingly weighty subject of waste disposal and environmental awareness, she explains.

"Designing a building and interior allows for a complete understanding of the client. From this intimacy the sense of humor and style is most easily expressed in the furnishings."

"As designers and architects we see the 'big picture' and are also able to see the holes in the market. I think we also lend a functional and structural eye to the design and fabrication."

"Good design is the product of function and fabrication integrated into the aesthetic."

"The designer's responsibility? Ergonomics, ecology, longevity, comfort...."

Apple. *Designed by Heather Faulding, 1993. Hand-beaten steel, patina finish. Optional upholstery for outdoor use. Available through Enza Inc. Photography by Lisa Bogden*

The Palm Tree. *Designed by Heather Faulding, 1993. Hand-beaten steel, patina finish. Optional upholstery for outdoor use. Available through Enza Inc. Photography by Lisa Bogden*

The Rhubarb Tree. *Designed by Heather Faulding and Margaret Davis, 1993. Hand-beaten steel, patina finish. Optional upholstery for outdoor use. Available through Enza Inc. Photography by Lisa Bogden*

Dhana Solish

"*I*am a second-generation designer," says Dhana Solish of Los Angeles. "I like to refer to myself as a 'Bauhaus baby'—the daughter of an urban planner who studied at the Chicago Institute of Design with Laslo Moholy-Nagy, Buckminster Fuller, and other seminal modernists. In the course of my upbringing and education, I went through the gamut of design styles, away from strict modernism into a more personally expressive variety of design."

Solish has been designing unique interiors and custom furniture in the Los Angeles area since 1988. She received her Master of Fine Arts from the University of California, Los Angeles, in Interior Design, and her Bachelor of Arts from the University of California, Santa Cruz in Aesthetic Studies. She has also studied at the Royal Academy of Art in the Netherlands and with Jorge Aulestia in Barcelona. She chose interior design, she says, because it seemed to be an area that could encompass all of her varied interests—environment, color, texture, light and furniture. "I also like the *useful* nature of the work. In my interiors work, I strive to articulate the spoken and unspoken needs and desires of my clients. It is truly a service business."

"*In furniture design, I am interested in the object, and I want to encode it with layers of intention and meaning. I think of my pieces as totems or talismans—reminders of place and objects that warrant repeated contemplation.*"

"*In making furniture, I have to confess that I feel most strongly about the design and resonance of a piece. However, each design is also a canvas for the study and interplay of form, color and material, as well as the answer to a set of functional parameters. I enjoy fine craftsmanship and wonderful materials—all these elements must be evenly matched to achieve a visually and functionally successful object.*"

"*As a designer, I am still under the utopian influence of the early avant garde. I feel strongly that designers today can perform a healing function in their work—reconnecting fragmented parts of our society. In my interiors, I de-emphasize the 'dis-topian' aspects of modern life. For example, in my L.A. Archetype Series, I tried to take several totemic aspects of Los Angeles and subtly incorporate them into functional objects that would counteract the impersonal vastness of the city by gently reminding us of where we are and why we came here. The back of each of the series' Silhouette Chairs represents a building type common to this city.*"

Segovia. *Designed and manufactured by Dhana Solish, 1988. Inspired by the classical guitar, it combines the instrument's forms and materials with a Cubist twist. Fabricated by Oswaldo Nakazato of solid maple and walnut. Photography by Philip Thompson*

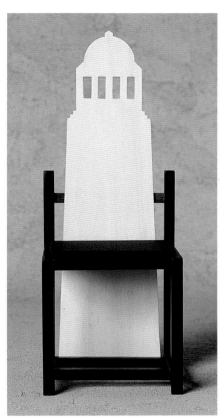

Campanile Chair

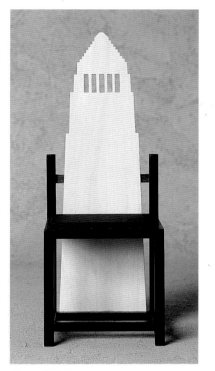

City Hall Chair

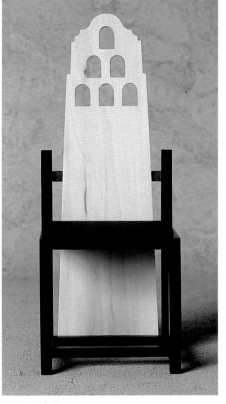

Mission Chair

Chinese Theater Chair

The Silhouette Chairs, *part of the L.A. Archetype Series. Designed by Dhana Solish, 1993. Fabricated by Cheryl Scott/Beachwood Canyon Woodworks of solid hardwoods, featuring mortise and tenon joinery. Black upholstery is standard.*
Photography by Philip Thompson

69

Scott Johnson

When architect Scott Johnson, partner in charge of design for Johnson Fain and Pereira Associates, Los Angeles, says he approaches the design of a piece of furniture as he does his buildings, it can make one wonder. After all, his buildings include such megastructures of Western urban skylines as the 650,000 square foot landmark Fox Plaza office building in Century City and the 1,000,000 square foot mixed-use Rincon Center, San Francisco. Yet they are also full of visual references to historical images so well entrenched in the collective unconscious that they universally evoke a sense of power and glory.

Immediately following Johnson's graduate studies at Harvard, he worked as a senior designer for The Architects Collaborative (TAC) in Boston, on a variety of commercial and institutional projects. Following that he moved to California where he opened the Los Angeles office for Skidmore, Owings & Merrill. He was an associate with Philip Johnson and John Burgee, Architects, New York City, from 1978 to 1983, the year he accepted his partnership at Johnson Fain and Pereira.

"I suppose I view furniture as a little architectural universe of its own. I want a chair or a table to do the work, and have object quality, but I also want it to evoke an attitude and a space (which is either the room, or it may be cerebral). I want it to suggest things beyond itself. We're talking about the power of idea here; much as we do in architecture.

"The three chairs here are very contemporary renditions of three historic chairs which I admire. Each is from an entirely different culture and the original means of construction and support of each is, of course, different. Nevertheless, I wanted to pare and edit them to what I consider their chief virtues. Also, I felt that in the twenty-first century everyone should be able to afford to sit in the King's seat. So we did them all in molded custom-finish plywood."

"The wonder of good furniture design is that it is not possible, except for purposes of dissection, to separate these qualities. There is no good design without a thorough, even transcendent knowledge of fabrication. And function of course is the essence of the piece: to sit, for example, and to inspire to sit."

"As life becomes inevitably more complex, our furniture will naturally reflect widening concerns. Whether we're talking sustainable hardwoods, occupational comfort, or making furniture for and by distant cultures, the best work will solve problems. Problems, however, are always being redefined."

Three Chairs. *Designed by Scott Johnson. Molded custom-finish plywood. Available through the architect. The simplest chair refers to a Pre-Hellenic chair originally done in hardwood and hemp, while the one with all the feet is based on a walnut Savonarola chair of the sixteenth century. The oval-backed chair with the gaudy front legs takes its cue from the classic Louis XVI chair marking the eclipse of royalty. Photography by Mark Lohman*

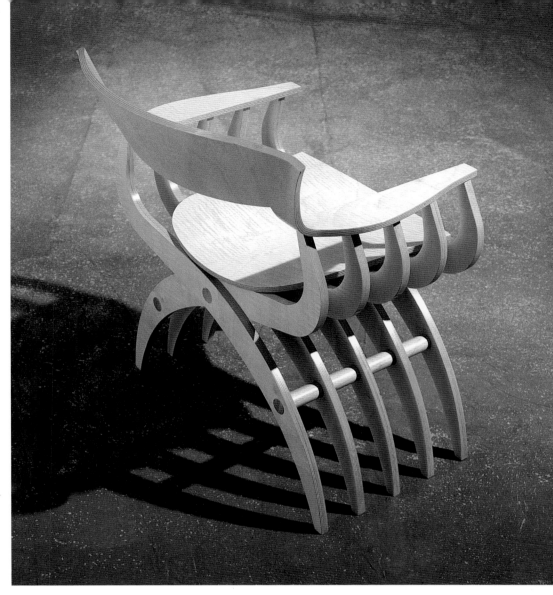

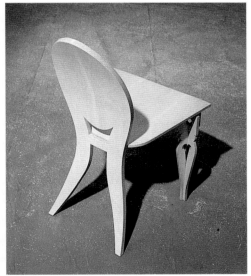

Christian Astuguevieille

"My approach to interior design came through my work as furniture designer," says Christian Astuguevieille. "My teaching was one as a pedagogue, first at the children's studio we developed at the Centre Georges Pompidou in Paris, and second at my own atelier which I created specifically for the needs of autistic children. These children had problems with elocution, so they needed the development of special techniques to reach them. For five years I worked with them on the ideas of tactility and the comprehension of space. That is how I started creating objects and furniture that would convey a strong sense of touch. Then friends and clients who liked my furniture asked me to create an atmosphere around them at their own homes."

Perhaps the lack of formal training was a godsend for this former artistic director of Rochas. Among sites of the frequent showings of his works for the past fifteen years have been: the Centre Georges Pompidou where he taught, the Musée des Arts Decoratifs, Galerie Yves Gastou and Galeria v.i.a. in Paris; Galerie Theoreme, Brussels; Galerie Ikon, London; and at the Richard Himmel showroom in Chicago and Turbulence Gallery in New York which represent his work in the United States. The Japanese also have been able to appreciate his work at Seibu/Ginza/Tokyo and at Comme des Garçons, Tokyo.

Chairs, Stools, and a Sellette.
From a collection designed by Christian Astuguevieille, 1990-1993. Rope or painted cotton cord over chestnut wood or, for some pieces, metal. Available through Eurl. Astuguevieille. Photographed in Christian Astuguevieille's atelier in Paris.

"Other than my work with the children at the Georges Pompidou Centre which gave me the idea to create extremely tactile objects, the only major influences on my work are the rituals of everyday life in so-called primitive civilizations. While doing research for the Musée des Arts Decoratifs in Paris, I had several journeys around Indonesia. Especially Balinese rituals and ceremonies have been an important source of inspiration for the choice of colors and materials in my work.

*"Last but not least my journeys to Japan have been a steady enrichment to my imagination. The Japanese sense of harmony pervading all aspects of life has influenced my perception of space and light. I learned as well the art of wrapping, the so-called art of **furoshiki**. I used this, in a modified European manner, on several occasions in my work—such as wrapping up the inside of Ungaro's couture house for the launching of the perfume Senso."*

"My responsibility seems to be to open people's minds and imaginations through my dream detonators and change their perception of everyday life. In a world where everything gets standardized, my purpose is to give people pieces with spirit and soul."

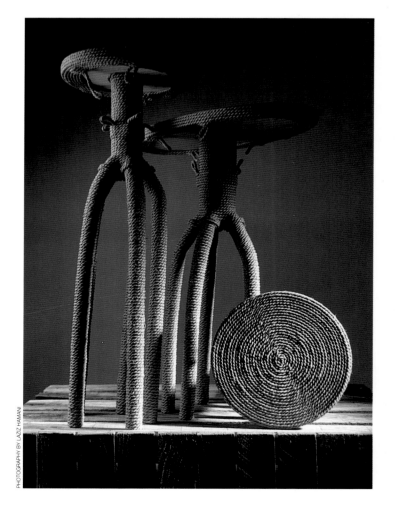

Kipp Stewart

*T*rained as an artist as well as an architect, Kipp Stewart is almost as well known for his paintings as for his designs, which have included the Ventana Inn and Restaurant in Big Sur, California, where he lives, and his outdoor teak furniture for Summit. Today he is concentrating his background in both fine art and design in a collaboration with his son in a new collection of wood, stone, steel and upholstered pieces that currently include chairs and tables, to which small cabinets and accessories eventually will be added. Every item in the hospitable array has been designed by Kipp Stewart and promoted through his own watercolor paintings. They are as evocative of the universal idea of simplicity and comfort as the furniture itself.

Stewart studied drawing, color, design, architecture and engineering at Chouinard Art Institute where he later taught. His furniture designs have been manufactured in the United States, Europe and Asia and have been used by major corporations, the United Nations, the Ford Foundation, The White House as well as hotels and residences throughout the world.

"I have come to see furniture as complementing spaces, not as tour de force, not clever or complex. I see the need for the simple line, for use and not for show."

"I cannot separate design and function. First, of course, comes comfort, then durability, and, only with care and much study, much trial and error, can a design result which has stature and dignity and perhaps be a handsome product."

"Comfort, long life, use of wood from sustained plantings ... all are responsibilities."

Dining Chair. *Designed by Kipp Stewart, 1993. Manufactured by Bradford Stewart & Company. Steel with clear powder coat, and oak slats with clear water finish. Suitable for outdoor as well as indoor use. Photography by Kipp Stewart*

Lenny Steinberg

The designs of Lenny Steinberg span two decades, every year in which she seemed to bring out surprisingly fresh ideas...colored glass and mirror furniture created with her partner Sara Binder for their company Vivid...concrete kitchens and baths...anodized aluminum and chrome jewelry. Now, in addition to current projects ranging from costume to graphics to interior design, she is working on the exhibition and production of her recent metal furniture and accessories.

"Most of the furniture I design is prompted by the architectural elements of a space. For example, in one recent project the furniture dimensions were based on the sixteen-inch-grid pattern of the stone floor. By designing furniture that corresponds to the heights and lines of the architecture I work to eliminate visual conflict, thereby creating strength and spatial harmony. Ultimately the pieces can live anywhere."

"Sometimes the impetus to design a piece is inspired by the properties and possibilities of a material. The challenge of fabrication turns heart to mind. Many thrilling ideas are thwarted by the mechanics of mechanics. Sometimes this is just one more step in the satisfying process of refinement.

"Function, for me, is a consideration of people...how a piece will be used and who will be using it. Continuing to imagine the visual and physical experience leads function back to form.

"So, finally, design, fabrication and function are a circle."

"Design is invention and reinvention. As with artists working in other disciplines, the designer is responsible for being true to his or her singular perspective. My view is that design, be it a chair or table or the whole space, should inspire the eye and stimulate the imagination."

Pony. *Designed by Lenny Steinberg, 1991. Shown in mirrored stainless steel. Also available in matte stainless steel and brushed steel. Seat: cotton (shown) or suede. Available through Lenny Steinberg Design Associates. Photography by George A. Sandoval*

Bi-Lateral. *Designed by Lenny Steinberg, 1989. Tilting backrest. Black matte laminate. Black leather. Available through Lenny Steinberg Design Associates. Photography by George A. Sandoval*

Anna Castelli Ferrieri

*T*he series of furniture which Anna Castelli Ferrieri has designed for Kartell results from a project spanning ten years of research in the field of new artificial materials and technologies. During this period the designer lived in intense contact with the operative reality of the Kartell company, which is almost unique in producing furniture items with a completely industrialized process. Her experiments were aimed at developing designs expressive of these new materials as well as exploitive of their peculiarities "in order to give them the dignity that any material gains when correctly used," she says.

Castelli Ferrieri studied at the University of Milano, where she earned a Master's degree in Architecture. In the early fifties, she served as assistant editor of the architectural review *Casabella Construzioni* and has been correspondent of the British review *Architectural Design*. She published a book

entitled *Plastics and Design*, Arcadia Ed., 1984, and a second book entitled *The Interfaces of Material*, Domus Academy Ed., 1991. A book, just published by Laterza and written by Cristina Morozzi, has been dedicated to Castelli Ferrieri's design work.

Castelli Ferrieri's professional activity ranges from town planning to industrial design, with particular regard to architecture, in the residential, industrial, commercial, religious and hospital fields. In addition to maintaining her own design office in Milan, she established, in 1990, ACF Officina, composed of an international group of designers whose exceptional talents and developed skills she has singled out while teaching at Domus Academy and Milan Polytechnic.

"I'm active both as an architect and as an industrial designer. I don't think the difference in scale may change my working method. Thus the two fields are strictly related from the formal viewpoint, too. I believe the architectural matrix is the most important, so my pieces of furniture are like small architectural works. They reveal their structure and the precise relationship among spaces."

"For me the most important thing is communicating with the user, thus interpreting his needs and his wishes. A product must meet the function it was designed for, be simple and essential, have a guaranteed duration and the right price. This is what I try to get when I design: it's the minimum requisite to get quality, but it's not enough. The remaining is the zest of emotionality I manage to convey just to communicate with the future user."

"The responsibility of the designer is quite big today. Each one of us must think twice before introducing a new piece of matter into the already overcrowded physical world and must ask himself whether that object really fills a need and whether it's innovative enough to justify its presence."

Multi-use Stools. Designed by Anna Castelli Ferrieri, 1979. Glass reinforced polypropylene seats, in four heights. Painted steel structure. Manufactured by Kartell. Winner of product design award by Resources Council USA 1979; selected for the Premio Compasso d'Oro ADI 1979; awarded gold medal at the BIO9 of Lubiana 1986.
Photography by Paolo Bolzoni

Armchair. Designed by Anna Castelli Ferrieri, 1992. Technopolymers blend. Manufactured by Kartell. Selected for the BIO13 of Lubiana 1992. Photography by Paolo Bolzoni

Small Stackable Stool-Table (Stooble). Designed by Anna Castelli Ferrieri, 1987. Polypropylene. Manufactured by Kartell. Received ICE Richtungsweisendes Design Award of the Möbelmesse Köln 1987; selected for the Premio Compasso d'Oro ADI 1987; selected for the Premio 5 stelle ADI Tecnhotel 1987; selected for the BIO12 of Lubiana 1988. Photography by Paolo Bolzoni

Tao Ho

*T*ao Ho received a Master of Architecture degree from Harvard University in 1964, then worked as personal assistant to Walter Gropius and Siegfried Giedion before returning to Hong Kong, where he set up his own multi-disciplinary TAOHO Design practice in 1968, combining architecture, urban design, interior and graphic design. In 1965 he was the first to introduce the Bauhaus Basic Design courses in Hong Kong.

Ho co-initiated and designed the award-winning Hong Kong Arts Centre. He received an Honorary Doctorate of Humane Letters from Williams College in 1979 in recognition of his energetic efforts to promote cultural activities in Hong Kong. During his twenty-five years of practice, Ho has been awarded numerous prizes including two Silver Medals and four Design Merits from the Hong Kong Institute of Architects.

In 1984, Ho co-founded the first and only Chinese Government approved joint-venture private architectural practice, Great Earth Architects &

Engineers International in Beijing, as a test model to reform architectural practice in China. Since then Tao Ho and Great Earth have been commissioned by the Chinese Government to plan and design three major cities: Xiamen, Qingdao, and Hangzhou.

In 1986, Ho won the international competition to design the Hong Kong Pavilion at Expo '86 in Vancouver. In 1989 he was commissioned to prepare a development strategy for the Government of Gibraltar. In 1991 he completed the Western Market revitalization which instantly became one of the most popular landmarks in Hong Kong. Other commissions of note include the renovation begun in 1993 of the 138-year-old Governor's Mansion in Hong Kong and the design of the flag and emblem of the Hong Kong Special Administrative Zone to be used after 1997.

"Being an architect and interior designer helps me to conceive the design of furniture either as part of the harmonious architectural/interior environment or as a piece of freestanding functional sculpture in space."

"To me, design, fabrication and function should be conceived as an integrated creative process from conception to production."

"A good design is a creative result in which ergonomics, ecology, longevity, economy and form are considered in a well-balanced manner."

THD Chair. *Designed by Tao Ho, 1973. Chromed steel pipe. Handmade prototype produced under the personal supervision of Tao Ho. Photography courtesy of Tao Ho*

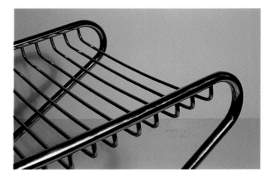

Juhani Pallasmaa

*D*ean of the Faculty of Architecture at Helsinki University of Technology, and head of his own architectural firm, professor Juhani Pallasmaa conducts a professional practice as broad as the subjects about which he teaches and writes. A few of his major recent projects have been the design of the Institut Finlandais, Paris; the continuing renovation of the KOP Bank City Block, Helsinki; and the continuing extension of the Court House in Kuopio, Finland. He has designed more than thirty exhibitions of Finnish architecture, town-planning and fine arts that have traveled the globe, as have his articles on the philosophy and theory of architecture and the visual arts. Awards have followed his invigorating example: He was honored as Knight of the Order of the White Rose of Finland in 1988, as Honorary Fellow of the American Institute of Architects in 1989, and received an Honorary Doctorate from Helsinki's University of Industrial Arts in 1993.

"All the objects I have designed have been conceived for specific contexts, i.e. they are extensions of my architectural ideas. Also my sculptural experiments are aspects of conceiving an aesthetical entity, a 'lifeworld' of sensory pleasure."

"For me, beauty has a definite moral value. When humanity stops longing for beauty, the sense of goodness and justice has been lost. I cannot detach various dimensions of design from the whole."

"The main responsibility of the designer is to project an ideal, a glimpse of a better world. In tomorrow's world, the most important criterion will be that of ecological performance. However, an aesthetics of precision and sensuality is a step toward a sensible ecological functionalism."

Side Chair, *prototype. Designed by Juhani Pallasmaa, 1991. Laminated plywood and carbon fiber, chromed spring steel. Not yet manufactured, only five prototype variations exist. Photography by Rauno Träskelin*

Frank O. Gehry

When the Knoll Group introduced its collection designed by world-renowned architect Frank O. Gehry, the firm premiered yet one more example of his unconventional application of materials and it was welcome.

Before founding his own firm in Santa Monica, California, Gehry received his Bachelor of Architecture degree from the University of Southern California and studied city planning at Harvard University's Graduate School of Design. He then apprenticed with architects Victor Gruen and Pereira & Luckman in Los Angeles and with André Remondet in Paris, beginning a career that spans three decades and has produced public and private buildings in America, Japan and, most recently, Europe.

"I've always been interested in furniture, probably because my dad had a little furniture company in Toronto for a while. And, architecture takes so long to make...that's why furniture is always so interesting to me. It's instant gratification. My experience as an architect selecting furniture for a client has been very disappointing. You go to the market and always find the same thing...a Mies chair. It's especially difficult for low budget projects. I would always wind up designing new furniture."

"With the Knoll furniture the strange thing is that everyone always likes the straight chairs. When they think of Gehry they think of neo-modern. Then they look at the Cross Check chair and say, 'Horrors! It looks decorative.' I didn't make it 'decorative.' Those swirls and curves are structural. If you look at Thonet chairs you see that all those curves are structural, even though they added an extra twirl or two to a curve. And the same is true in my chairs. All of the bentwood furniture to this point—Thonet's, Aalto's, and Eames'—always had a heavy sub-structure and then webbing, or an intermediary structure for the seating. The difference in my chairs is that the support structure and the seat are formed of the single lightweight slender wood strips, which serve both functions. The material forms a single and continuous idea. What makes all this work and gives extraordinary strength is the interwoven, basket-like character of the design.

"Now structure and material have freed bentwood furniture from its former heaviness and rigidity. It really is possible to make bentwood furniture pliable, springy and light."

High Sticking Side Chair.

Photography by Jay Ahrend

The Gehry Collection. *Designed by Frank O. Gehry, 1992. Manufactured by The Knoll Group.*
Laminated strips of U.S. grown maple harvested from sustainable forests. The water-based dip finish is also environmentally sound. Named after ice hockey terms reflecting the designer's passion for the sport of his native Canada, the collection is available in: Hat Trick Side Chair (with arms and armless); High Sticking Side Chair; Cross Check Lounge Chair; Power Play Lounge Chair with Offside Ottoman; Face Off Table; Icing Table.

Hat Trick Chair.

Photography by Tim Street-Porter

Cross Check Chair with pad.

Photography by Jay Ahrend

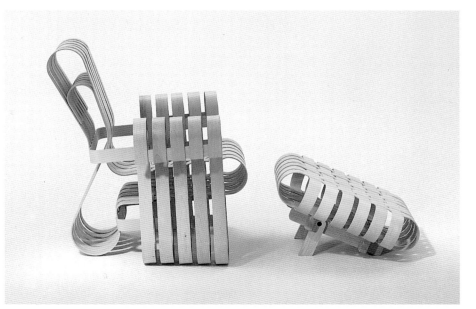

Hat Trick Chair.

Photography by Jay Ahrend

Power Play Chair and **Offside Ottoman**.

Photography by Jay Ahrend

Thomas A. Heinz

*O*ver the years, Thomas A. Heinz has become a nationally recognized authority on America's foremost modern architect, Frank Lloyd Wright. Heinz's extensive background as a residential and commercial architect has afforded him the rare opportunity to work on forty Wright buildings and to install the Frank Lloyd Wright Room at the Metropolitan Museum of Art in New York. In addition, he has written nine books on Wright, one of the latest being on his furniture. The painstaking research that has gone into these projects, exemplified by the more than fifty thousand photographs he has compiled on Wright's work, has also gone into the reproductions of Wright's furniture by Heinz & Co., the company he founded in Evanston, Illinois, in 1975. Yet without having been an architect himself, he says, he probably would not have appreciated to the same extent Wright's accomplishments.

"Understanding structural design and being aware of proportion is essential in furniture design. Some furniture is built-in, other pieces are large—both factors sometimes obscuring the line between furniture and architecture. The furniture has to obey the laws of nature and at the same time it has to appear to do what it is intended to do. Chairs support people vertically and horizontally. Tables support only in the vertical direction. The choices of materials and colors are as important in furniture as they are in architecture. Designs in the Heinz & Co. line were not reproduced based on market but rather to fit in a harmonious interior. It is surprising that these turn-of-the-century designs are equally comfortable in modern and period interiors."

"Design, fabrication and function are all of equal value. All of these factors have to be completely satisfied in order to be a finished product. One cannot be thought of out of context to the others."

"Architects and furniture designers are responsible for everything. This begins with the problem of shipping and installing each piece. They must be able to get through doors and arrive in undamaged condition. The pieces themselves are intended to last indefinitely if properly cared for by the client/owner. Design, comfort and utility are key factors when designing."

Reclining Spindle Chair. Designed by Frank Lloyd Wright, 1906. Reproduced by Thomas A. Heinz. Manufactured by Heinz & Co. Quarter-sawn, solid oak. Available with covers of wool or leather, eight standard finishes or custom finish.

"The reclining spindle chair is a variation on a popular design by architect Philip Webb which was based on the Morris Chair, named after William Morris of England, the founder of the Arts & Craft Movement of which Wright and Stickley were very much a part," says Heinz. "The Morris and Webb designed chair is adjusted by the movement of a bar behind the back of the chair. Wright's chair is based on the same principle but the adjustment is hidden under the seat.

"Wright designed many variations of this chair, utilizing different inset, vertical, horizontal panels, but the arms of Wright's chairs varied little and the dimensions of the inserts and slides were common to all."

Photography by Thomas A. Heinz

Spindle Couch. *Designed by Frank Lloyd Wright, 1912. Reproduced by Thomas A. Heinz. Manufactured by Heinz & Co. Quarter-sawn, solid oak. Available with covers in wool or leather, and eight standard finishes or custom finish. Photographed with some of the thirty other Wright designs reproduced by Heinz & Co., on view in the showroom of the dealer, Porter's of Racine, Wisconsin.*
Photography by Thomas A. Heinz

Antti Nurmesniemi

*F*urniture by Finland's Antti Nurmesniemi has become part of the collections of almost as many museums as private households. Among those documenting our times with his richly human, intelligently engineered designs are the Metropolitan Museum of Art and the Museum of Modern Art in New York; the Philadelphia Museum of Art in Philadelphia; the Stedelijk Museum in Amsterdam; the Die Neue Sammlung in Munich, the Malmö Museum in Malmö (Sweden); the Oslo Museum of Applied Art and the Finnish Museum of Applied Arts. Yet he

also has long been drawn to other areas of design, as evidenced by his 1984 telephone for Fujitsu and his 1988 paper-reel wraps for Enso Oy, reflecting on the one hand his interest in high technology and, on the other hand, in design aimed at a broad consumer base. Indeed, it is these two interests with which one might seek to define the special qualities seen even in his chairs and tables.

"I have always worked in a very close relationship to architecture and at the same time designed interiors. Most of my furniture designs have been made for a specific building. In such a situation, the requirements of architecture are seen in form of scale and general intellectualism. As for free industrial product design, current trends and the possibilities which technology provides fulfill the designer's creative work more than a built environment (i.e. architecture) does."

"Function, fabrication and design together form one entity. The aim always should be a harmony between these elements."

"At the very least a designer is responsible for the aspects of his profession which pertain to a project. Under the best circumstances, however, a designer can have a very wide influence not only within but also outside his own professional field."

Dining Table Chair. *Designed by Antti Nurmesniemi, 1991. Oak and alcantara upholstery in seat and back. Manufactured by Puusepänliike Nurmi. A 1985 version was of painted birch with cotton upholstery. Manufactured by Puulon Oy.*
Photography by Ilmari Kostiainen

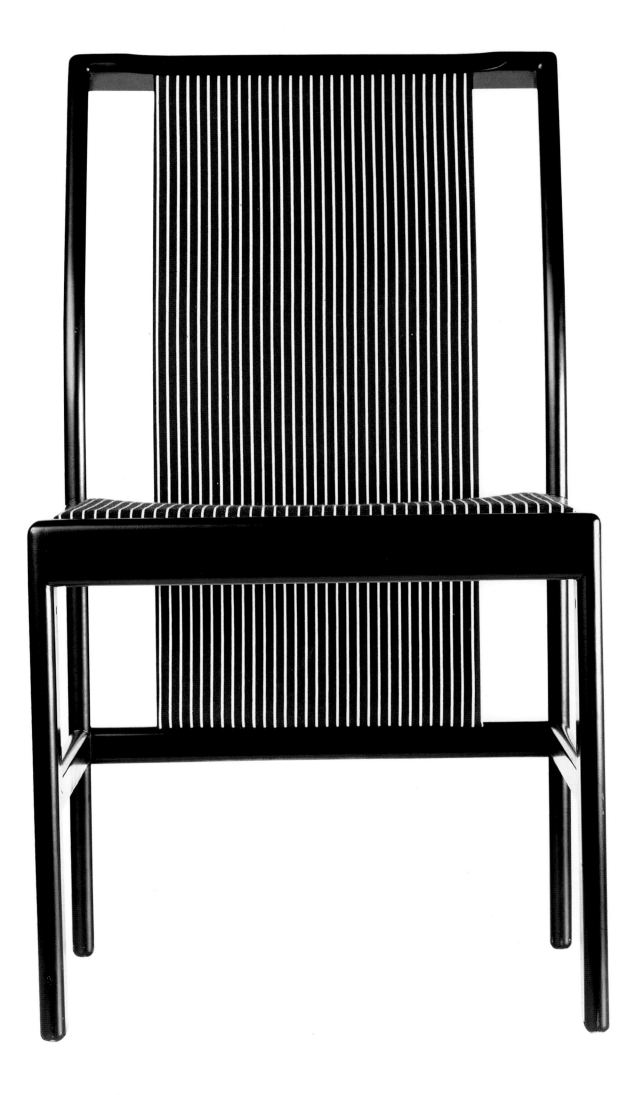

Javier Mariscal

*J*avier Mariscal started drawing underground comics in the early seventies. He also developed a variety of projects including posters, logos, painting and sculpture, and the Garriris soon emerged as his favorite characters.

In the eighties, Mariscal focused on designing bars and interiors, ceramics, fabrics, rugs and furniture. Estudio Mariscal was established in 1989 in order to accomplish the task of developing Cobi, the mascot for the Barcelona Olympic Games. Corporate Cobis were developed along with their three-dimensional prototypes. Posters and limited silk-screen editions were designed, as well as applications for several different products. The studio brought Cobi to life, surrounding him with friends and providing him with a world of his own that was further developed in the cartoon series "The Cobi Troupe" and a series of six comic books. All the work developed around Cobi was compiled in *The Cobi Book*, published in 1992.

Estudio Mariscal's strongest point has been the development of its own style of animation, and in 1992 five books on Mariscal's work were pub-

lished in Japan, Germany, the United Kingdom and Spain.

From September 1992 to March 1993, in collaboration with the architect Alfredo Arribas, Estudio Mariscal developed Acuarinto for the Huis ten Bosch theme park in Nagasaki, Japan. The project consists of a space with a central maze whose walls are filled with water, surrounded by monitors playing interactive games for children. The interactive animation, 55 feet wide, combines three-dimensional backgrounds with two-dimensional animated cartoon characters. A line of merchandising products, including three hundred items, was also designed, based on the three standard manuals developed by Estudio Mariscal.

Estudio Mariscal now includes a team of twenty people (animators, graphic designers, sculptors and management). Over the past four years, they have designed three hundred forty-seven different graphic design, interior design and animation projects.

> "I have always worked in a wide range of the fields of art and design. It is always a question of working with images and translating these images into different materials and shapes."

> "The most important thing for me is the design itself—playing with shapes and materials."

> "I think of my work as communication. My responsibility is to create items that make the lives of others happier."

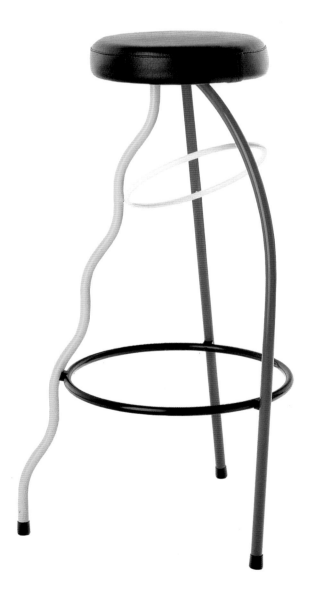

Duplex. *Designed by Javier Mariscal, 1983. Produced by B.D. Ediciones de Diseño. Painted steel and leather. Photography courtesy of Estudio Mariscal*

Garriri. Designed by Javier Mariscal, 1987. Produced by Akaba. Iron, aluminum and leather.
Photography courtesy of Estudio Mariscal

M.O.R. Sillon. Designed by Javier Mariscal, 1986. Produced by Akaba. Iron, fabric and leather.
Photography courtesy of Estudio Mariscal

Pulpo Pirata. Exclusively designed in iron and produced by Javier Mariscal in 1988 for the restaurant Gambrinus in Barcelona.
Photography courtesy of Estudio Mariscal

Kisho Kurokawa

*F*or the past thirty years Kisho Kurokawa has reflected in his work what he sees as the paradigm shift from the Age of the Machine principle to the Age of Life principle, the key concepts of which he calls Metabolism, Metamorphosis and Symbiosis. In his numerous articles as well as his widely awarded book, *The Philosophy of Symbiosis*, he has probed the interrelationship between time and space, man and technology, man and nature, one culture and another, and how they are or might be influenced by Buddhism and traditional concepts in Japanese culture.

Born in Nagoya in 1934, Kurokawa received his architectural degree at Kyoto University. In 1960 while doing postgraduate work for his doctorate at Tokyo University, he formed, with several other people, the "Metabolist Group" which advocated that the city and architecture are an organism capable of growth and change based on Buddhist philosophy.

Much awarded, Kurokawa most recently received the 1990 Prize of Architectural Institute of Japan for Hiroshima City Museum of Contemporary Art and the 1992 Prize of Japan Art Academy for Nara City Museum of Photography.

"My theory towards architecture, especially the symbiosis of history and the future, is as important as a concept to me when designing furniture as when designing a building. This Edo Series furniture introduces the Japanese traditional forms into the modern furniture by finishing with the lacquer."

*"The most important thing is the **balance** of the design, the production and the function."*

"My intention is for everything I design to reflect the richness afforded through a recognition of the plurality of life. In the Age of Life principle the rising interest in the environment and the new importance given ecology aim at preserving the diversity of life. Everything on earth is linked to all cultures, languages, traditions and arts, but they should be connected in a symbiotic way that celebrates individuality rather than the universality idealized in the recent past by the machine age. The design of furniture as well as of architecture should be open to all regional and urban contexts, nature and the environment.

"Symbiosis is essentially different from harmony, compromise, amalgamation or eclecticism. Symbiosis is made possible by recognizing reverence for the sacred zone between different cultures, opposing factors, different elements, between the extremes of dualistic opposition."

Lounge Chair. *Timber frame and legs; frame finished with green, vermilion and black lacquer; legs finished with aluminum paint; brass connectors; seat covered with black leather.*

Armchairs. *Matte urethane paint finish, cloth covered cushion.*

Edo Series. Designed by Kisho Kurokawa in 1982, with the exception of the Lounge Chair commissioned two years later for the lobby of the Roppongi Prince Hotel. Lacquered and painted wood. Produced and distributed by Consonni. Photography courtesy Kisho Kurokawa Architect & Associates

High-back Chair. Lacquer finish, leather covered seat.

Dining Chairs. Matte urethane paint finish, cloth covered seat.

89

Mario Botta

*H*aving worked in the studio of Le Corbusier and later with Louis Kahn, the revered architect, Mario Botta opened his own architecture office in Lugano in 1969, from there conducting his worldwide design, teaching and research activities. Current projects include: the new Museum of Modern Art in San Francisco; the cathedral in Evry, France; Union Bank of Switzerland building in Basel, Switzerland; the museum of modern art in Roverto, Italy; the telecommunications center in Bellinzona, Switzerland; administrative buildings in Lugano, Switzerland; churches in Mogno, Switzerland, and Merate, Italy; a chapel on Mount Tamaro, Switzerland; and a museum for the works of Jean Tinguely in Basel, Switzerland.

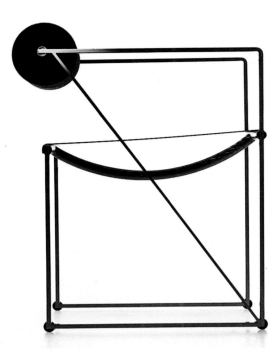

"What motivates the architect to draw, or rather to re-draw, objects we use every day? The objects that surround us and the spaces we build every day around us represent our hopes, speak of our sensibilities and are positive witnesses of our times. Everyday objects, banal objects, are the closest to our habits and bring us closest to our fellow men. These objects create a bond between all of us. They offer us discreet occasions for quiet dialogues, they maybe, even in spite of ourselves, attract us. In our everyday lives, it is not easy to avoid a chair, a table, a lamp. That is why it is best, perhaps, to consider pieces of furniture as friendly objects, quite capable of talking to us, telling us a multitude of little secrets.

"For the architect all this signifies a confrontation with the 'already made' and the 'already seen' and challenges a new interpretation. Every new project is a reassessment that becomes an unavoidable 'correction-destruction' of a given object. Quite often it is not the function or the usage of the object that changes, but simply the meaning, acquiring new connotations and needs. Thus, the meaning of things, their deepest content, is hidden behind the use the object was created for."

"To re-draw an object is also a way to confront our era, as it forces the designer to search the past of an object and to draw from history. This process involves trying to give meaning to shapes and materials used, the pleasure of rediscovering the beauty of simple and ancient work and trades, the satisfaction of finding logic in the rules of assembling a piece, finding a cost-effective way to manufacture, using the least to obtain the most. For the architect this process of creation is richer and more gratifying than the finished work."

Seconda Chair, *1982, shown with Terzo Table, 1983. Designed by Mario Botta. Manufactured by Alias Spa. Seconda Chair: Epoxy enamelled steel structure and connecting bars. Pressed steel seat, enamelled in metallized silver or dull black. Black constituted by rotating cylindrical elements realized in soft expanded polyurethane in dark gray. Four cylindrical supports in a dull black stiff plastic.*
Photography by Aldo Ballo

Yrjö Kukkapuro

*T*he special vision of Professor Yrjö Kukkapuro continues to educate and illuminate others who are interested in design not only through his appointments to teach about architecture and the industrial arts at leading Finnish schools and universities but also through his designs themselves. They are now in the permanent collections of museums in Europe, the United States and the Middle East…and they are being annually unveiled in a continuous thread of excellence, as shown in his 1993 Alnus chairs and table for Avarte.

"Modern furniture design reflects modern architecture. Functions and aesthetic values are generated through modern architecture."

"Deepest down in design the designer is striving after the best possible products. That is the human approach. In the present economic situation, the responsibility to the working community has been emphasized. Designers are members of a working community trying to do their best competing with themselves and their colleagues."

"Regarding the responsibility of the designer, the operational function, especially in operational articles manufactured in series production, is important. The ergonomics are important and also the ecological thinking from the aspect of protection of the surroundings has to be considered. Long-lasting products, energy and technology used in production, material savings…all are utmost!"

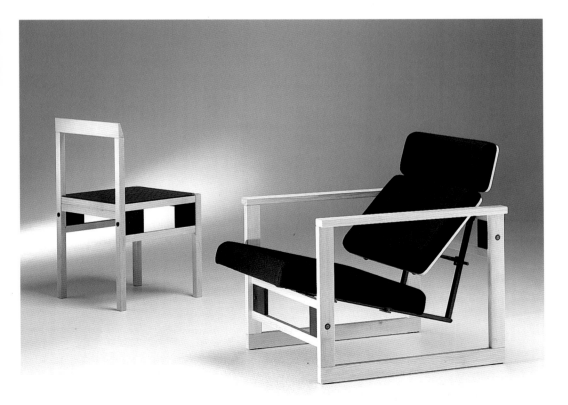

Alnus Chair and Easy Chair.
Designed by Yrjö Kukkapuro, 1993. Manufactured by Avarte Oy. Transparent black alder with water-based furniture lacquer. Seating: curly birch with black supporting units. Also in the collection: the Alnus dining table, designed by Yrjö Kukkapuro and Kari Korvenranta. Tabletop of solid natural wood or chipboard covered with high pressure laminate, edges and feet of solid alder, horizontal supports of transparent black stained alder covered with water-based furniture lacquer. Tabletop also can be covered with alder veneer. Both chairs and table are knockdown furniture providing the possibility for stocking and transporting in pieces that still are easy to assemble without special skills or tools. Photography by Marco Melander/Kimmo Virtanen

Mark Singer

*M*ark Singer, who founded Giati Designs in Santa Barbara in 1991, brings to the furniture he manufactures twenty-five years of experience in the industry. He has taught at Harvard University, apprenticed under master craftsman Sam Maloof, and designed and manufactured specific products for other companies and institutions in the U.S. and overseas. While Mark Singer Design Studios (MSDS) continues as the research arm for Giati as well as for product invention (such as water saving devices and support structures), it also provides real estate renovation and residential restoration services.

Singer's furniture was selected for display and sale at the New York Museum of Modern Art in 1986 and 1987, and at the San Francisco Museum of Modern Art in 1988.

"The architecture of our homes should be an expression of ourselves. The problem is that we usually design, own, and build very few homes in our lifetime and it is so difficult to get it right.

"It is much easier to design, build and remake full size working prototypes of furniture than it is to redesign and rebuild homes.

"Therefore, the design, proportions and detailing of our furniture should be a more perfect expression of ourselves. We hand furniture down from generation to generation, and we collect, keep and carry our favorite furniture as we move from residence to residence. The result is that furniture can serve as a bridge between the architecture of our home and a more representative expression of ourselves."

"Design, function and fabrication should not be separated from the design process. An understanding of the physical properties of materials and the ability to work with them and fabricate one's own prototypes are essential elements of and enrich the design process."

"A designer's responsibility should extend beyond the 'visual delight.'

"The responsible usage of raw materials (e.g. using plantation grown woods) and environmentally sound manufacturing processes should be as important to the designer as product safety, function and form.

"Because our natural resources are finite, inexpensive furniture constructed primarily from petroleum-based products is ecologically unsound and should be recycled or redesigned and made to last a lifetime.

"Unfortunately, though understandable, there is a very large market for the $4.99 resin chair."

Experimental Executive Chair.

Designed by Mark Singer, 1982. Cast aluminum, walnut and leather.

Photography courtesy of Mark Singer

Lounge Chair. *Designed by Mark Singer, 1985. Special order through MSDS Designs. Metal frame, fiberglass shell, leather cushions.*
Photography courtesy of Mark Singer

Dining/Side Chair. *Designed by Mark Singer, 1980. Manufactured by Giati Designs, Inc. American black walnut, Knoll wool.*
Photography courtesy of Mark Singer

Armchair, Lounge Chairs, Ottoman and Side Table from the Paradiso Collection. *Designed by Mark Singer, 1989. Manufactured by Giati Designs, Inc. Natural teak, solution dyed acrylic fabric.*
Photography courtesy of Giati Designs

Thayer Hopkins

*T*hayer Hopkins returned to the San Francisco Bay area in 1975 after receiving a Bachelor of Fine Arts degree and a Bachelor of Architecture degree from the Rhode Island School of Design, where he

studied furniture design as well. He has practiced architecture in association with the firm of Fee Munson Ebert since 1985, and maintains an independent practice as consulting designer for clients including The Wicker Works in San Francisco, whose designs by Hopkins are featured here. His completed work includes a variety of residential, retail, commercial, corporate and educational projects, as well as diverse commissions ranging from stage sets to the design of spaces on board an aircraft carrier. In addition to his award-winning furniture, he has designed product, packaging and graphic identity programs.

"The process of creating furniture is a more focused enterprise than orchestrating the design of an entire building. It provides a welcome change of pace and scale. It allows me to go back into the workshop and to have more direct contact with materials. It is not only refreshing to be able to work in both areas, but also important for my growth. I get frustrated by the current arbitrary and prejudicial notions which seem to divide architecture, interiors and furniture. These are all interrelated aspects of the same fundamental activity, which is the creation of places that respond to the complexities of our existence in a physical world, hopefully transcending functionality to express and enrich our humanity."

"The preeminence of design, fabrication or function varies with each object and is determined by the intended use, the materials from which the piece will be made, and in large part by the preference of the designer. Residential furniture design in general allows an enormous latitude for personal expression; it is driven far less by strict requirements of function than would be the design of an office work chair, for example. The separation of these qualities is a semantic abstraction though, for in great design all are served in the same solution."

"Designers are faced with increasingly manifest responsibilities in a world in which finite resources serve an expanding population. We live in an environment largely of our own creation, reflecting all the great achievements of design as well as the failures and deficiencies. As our understanding of the ethics of our consumption grows, this general awareness produces an evermore discriminating user. This is an encouraging direction, and demands more of us as designers."

The Hopkins Rope Collection.
Designed by Thayer Hopkins, 1991-1992. Abaca handwoven into rope, over wood with wrought iron. Manufactured by The Wicker Works. Collection includes dining side chair, dining armchair, barstool, lounge chair and ottoman, loveseat, and dining table. Photography by Colin McRae

Warren Snodgrass

Warren Snodgrass is president of Design Technology, an industrial design firm whose studio is located on San Francisco Bay. He worked for the architectural firm of William Pereira and Associates, later served as senior project designer with architect Charles Luckman, and still later as director of design for the San Francisco office of Selje, Bond and Stuart before founding his own firm in 1975. He credits in part his extensive background in architectural design and space planning for the success of his furniture designs for various manufacturers including Steelcase, Thonet, Haworth, Tropitone, and Stow & Davis.

A graduate of Art Center College of Design, Snodgrass has received design awards from the American Institute of Architects, the Resources Council, the American Institute of Interior Designers, and the Institute of Business Designers. Among his award-winning designs are the Continuum Stacking Chair, the Free Dimensional Open Plan System, and the Interlock Stacking Chair. Recent introductions include the Snodgrass Collection for Steelcase and the Catalyst chair series for Haworth.

"A background in interior design and architecture has made me acutely aware of what specifiers and end users are looking for in the furniture market."

"Like almost everything else in life, the key to success in furniture design is a balance of all the critical elements. Function is paramount. We first define the problems we intend to solve and then make sure the design can be built economically. The aesthetics are a result of painstaking attention to detail."

"A design is as good or as bad as its weakest element. If we do our job correctly, every facet of the design has been resolved successfully, and ecological responsibility is one of these facets."

Perception Chair. *Designed by Warren Snodgrass. Introduced by Tropitone in 1989. All aluminum. Photography by John Svoboda*

Continuum Chair. *Designed by*
Warren Snodgrass, and introduced by
Stow & Davis, a division of Steelcase, in
1980. Laminated wood.
Photography by Bruce Wolf

Otto Zapf

*F*or the past two decades Otto Zapf has worked from offices both in his native Germany and in the United States, launching designs that have had widespread impact in the office furnishings field particularly... but not exclusively. From his own widely published homes to his no-nonsense but highly articulate, functional and aesthetically sensitive furniture, his influence has been felt in the home as well. Indeed, it is not possible to forecast which sector will benefit most from the new Contur chairs he has introduced through Design Trade, a limited partnership recently formed with his wife Roselie and his son Florian.

"These chairs have a special suspended 'tongue' incorporated into the backrest that moves forward to give full support at all times, during any changes of position," says Otto Zapf. "This back support follows the body automatically, with no levers or knobs needed. So these chairs not only are comfortable for hours, but they don't have that mechanical look that keeps many chairs considered for office use only."

"I started in 1969 as an interior designer with my own showroom. I designed homes, shops, exhibitions...and found myself using more and more the furniture that I would design myself. To me, designing the entire interior, including the furniture, is the ultimate."

"Design reaches its maximum when form, function and price are in balance."

"In my opinion, the main responsibility of a designer is to serve people—then comes everything else, including aesthetics."

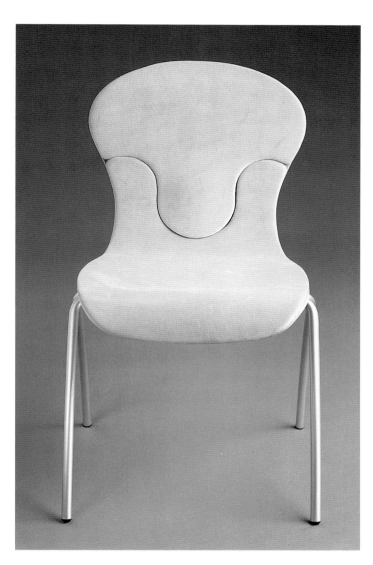

Contur. *Designed by Otto Zapf, 1993. Manufactured by Design Trade. Pressed beech plywood, impregnated hard wax finish. Available with two leg variations, armrests (left or right and upholstered or plywood finish). Legs and armrests of powder-coated steel, silverlight or silver-dark. Full or partial upholstery available. Vertical stacking possible with four-leg version and with all three armrest variations.*

Photography by Michael Lehmann

Paul Haigh

*H*aigh Architects, headquartered in Greenwich, Connecticut, is a firm committed to achieving an understanding between design disciplines, and its portfolio of projects represents a multi-disciplined approach to architecture, interior architecture and furniture design on an international level. English-born Paul Haigh, who founded the firm with his partner Barbara H. Haigh in 1981, sees the development of this approach as a legacy from his training and experience in Europe, where the professional boundaries between architecture and design seem less specialized than in practice in the United States. This multi-disciplinary attitude has led to a perception of the Haigh Studio work as both ironic and practical with a high degree of design rigor. By his rejection of the notion of professional boundaries, his design experience has been widened to offer solutions and ask questions through influences and research in many different disciplines.

"Rather than my being an architect influencing my furniture design, I find the reverse—that being a furniture designer has affected my perspective as an architect. The role of scale, detail and use of materials is so condensed in the creation of a furniture piece that my way of looking at the same issues in architecture has been changed significantly. My work in furniture design is for mass production. The level of detail demanded by this process alters one's perspective on the refinement to be attained in architectural work."

"I see no separation between design, fabrication and function. Design, by my definition, should embrace all these issues to offer solutions and sometimes ask newer questions."

"The designer has a responsibility to the culture. If the designer's life and intellect are balanced, the cognizance of the design work will be apparent."

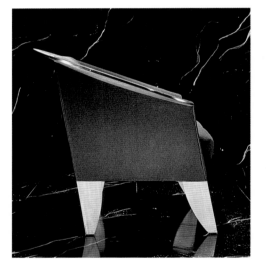

Enigma. *Designed by Paul Haigh, 1987. Manufactured by Bernhardt. Wood veneer. Upholstered seat and back cushion available in textile or leather. Photography courtesy of Bernhardt*

Sinistra Left and Right Armchairs. *Designed by Paul Haigh, 1987. Manufactured by Bernhardt. Wood veneer. Upholstered seat cushion available in textile or leather. Photography courtesy of Bernhardt*

Janice Feldman

*I*nterior designer Janice Feldman is owner and founding president of JANUS et Cie, a high quality service-oriented distributor of furnishings and textiles and located in the Pacific Design Center, Los Angeles. Feldman, who personally selects everything in her showroom with an eye toward design excellence, is a bright, creative, successful woman whose energy reflects her never-ending quest to make this world a better place. It only seemed natural that, in this time of concern about overcrowded landfills, shrinking timberland and the future of our planet earth, she

would be among those using their creativity to develop furniture from recycled materials—in her case, milk jugs.

Feldman also is an independent interior designer, carousel restorer and historian, graphic designer, painter, printmaker, teacher, writer and photographer. In addition, she is a founding member of ADPSR (Architects, Designers, and Planners for Social Responsibility) and serves on the Board of Governors of the Pacific Design Center, where she dedicated The Murray Feldman Gallery in memory of her late husband.

"Being a designer with a broad base of education and cultural exposure allows me to envision many options as to where and how my products may be used. The great challenge is not only to come up with innovative ideas but also to accept that there may be another use for the piece which I have not yet discovered."

"I would have to say that function is the most important thing. If an object is the finest design in the world to be used in a practical context and it does not function, its value is worthless...unless, of course, its purpose is solely as a work of art. This is another matter altogether.

"The challenge of this, especially to those of us who are sensitive to art and design, is that we are often initially attracted to things by their design and not by their function."

"All these issues of responsibility...ergonomics, ecology, longevity...have their place. They may be mutually exclusive or interdependent depending on why the piece is being made in the first place.

"In the case of my Windsong rocker, it is clearly not an innovative design. It is a classic idea that has been interpreted thousands of times in countless materials. What is truly original about it is the material. The inspiration was to take an object that was universally familiar and simple to understand...apple pie, milk and cookies and so forth. People would immediately be attracted to it because it is familiar. Once they touch it, sit in it, or just read about what it is made of, their reaction is eternally different.

"Our base material is composed of 100 percent recycled high density polyethylene (HDPE) derived from purified milk bottle waste. We infuse color into the material and extrude it into lumber."

Windsong Rocker. *Designed by Janice Feldman, 1993. From a collection of interior and exterior products fabricated out of JANUSwood (a material made from purified discarded milk containers). Available through JANUS et Cie. Photography courtesy of JANUS et Cie.*

Norman Sukkar

Norman Sukkar entered the field of design through a background in the visual arts, receiving a Master of Fine Arts degree from Pratt Institute in New York City in 1977. His work is part of museum, gallery and private collections throughout the world. At a 1984 exhibit of his photographs and paintings of interiors was a couple who had just purchased a 3,000 square foot loft. On viewing Sukkar's artwork, they asked if he would consider helping them design their space. He consented,

enjoyed it immensely, and since then has been continuously designing interiors, exteriors, landscapes and furnishings, several of which he began producing in 1991.

Sukkar's work is in the permanent collection of the Cooper-Hewitt National Design Museum in New York City. His clients include Saks Fifth Avenue and Polo/Ralph Lauren. He headquarters both his furniture and his design groups in New York City.

"Being a furniture designer affects my perspective as an environmental designer as much as being an environmental designer affects my furniture. I think of my furniture on its own but I tend to think of space in terms of my furniture. That sounds quite limiting. I'll tell you why it's not. First, because limitations are the springboards of creativity. And second, it often happens that a new piece arises from a new space, a new project, a certain vista, an architectural element, a color in nature, a synthetic color, a certain client, a project site, and so on, and so on. My space is a victim of the elements that go into it."

"What's most important—design, fabrication or function? This is tricky. Five years ago I wouldn't have hesitated to say Design (with a capital D). Now it's not so simple. I'm being asked more and more to create cheaper (or should I say 'less expensive') products. Or to reduce cost of the pieces already created. So when Saks Fifth Avenue gives us a large order for a table, chair, or what-have-you, and then gives a large order to reduce the price (which, five years ago, was unheard of), we begin to think a lot about fabrication.

"As far as function goes, the old 'form follows function' edict is a casualty of the new economics. Actually, I believe that even among the keenest zealots of that philosophy the reverse was and is mostly true. Function follows form, as it should be, as it was, as it always will be."

"There is so much more involved with designing now. Not only do we have to concern ourselves with designing in reverse (going from fabrication and production to concept and design), but we must also prefigure any and every possible cosmic dilemma. We must also worry about the poor, the rich, the land, the water, the sky, the children, the physically challenged, the human anatomy. Yet we do have a historical responsibility and I strive to live up to that. Meaning: these things, extraneous to design, must be respected but not at the cost of the aesthetic—which is the primary responsibility of the designer."

Square Chair. *Designed by Norman Sukkar, 1992. From the Square Series which includes a side table/ottoman, bench, stool, console. Available through the designer in custom sizes, materials, finishes, colors. Thin gauge aluminum. Part of the permanent collection of the Cooper-Hewitt National Design Museum, New York City.*

*"The Square Chair came about at a construction site. We were doing a corrugated room and the bends, purposeful and otherwise, intrigued me. In no time this chair was on paper in its first form. Next, a prototype. Then, to make it more comfortable (and it **is** comfortable), I used the thinnest gauge aluminum that would not fatigue so the back would have a rocking effect. I also played with the angles of the front and back for ergonomics."—**Norman Sukkar** Photography courtesy of Norman Sukkar Design Group*

Triality Chair. *Designed by Norman Sukkar, 1991. From the Triality Series which includes a table with leaf, bookcase, children's table and chair, other custom options. Made of veneered plywood. Available through the designer in all materials, finishes, colors.*

*"The Triality Series simply came from a client who wanted everything in threes. We designed his loft with triangular rooms, three windows to each outside wall, kid's room with a triangular bed, desk, bookcase and chairs. Limitations made for a challenging and, in the end, wonderful project."—**Norman Sukkar***

Photography courtesy of Norman Sukkar Design Group

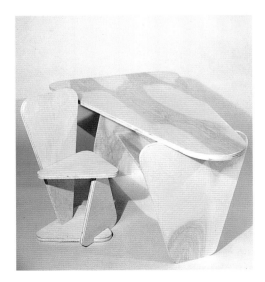

Warren Platner

Warren Platner has carried on a broad practice of design in his own name in New Haven, Connecticut, since 1965. His work in interior design, in product design, and in architecture has included offices, hotels, restaurants, ships, schools, showrooms, shopping centers, libraries, research laboratories and residences. His work has been used to illustrate hundreds of books (such as *The Office Book, Creating an Interior, Dining by Design, More Places for People, Ten by Warren Platner*) and magazines internationally and has been shown in such museums as the Louvre in Paris and the Museum of Modern Art in Rio de Janeiro.

His personal awards include the Interior Design Hall of Fame, the Graham Foundation Award for Advanced Studies in The Fine Arts, New York Designers Lighting Forum Award, President's Fellow of Rhode Island School of Design, Rome Prize in Architecture, the Advanced Research Fulbright Award in Architecture and Fellow of the American Institute of Architects.

Among Platner's well-known works in the field of interior design are headquarters offices for Sea Containers and the Pan Am Building public spaces; Water Tower Place in Chicago and shopping centers in the heart of Atlanta; Windows on the World restaurant; The Lodge at Vail, Colorado, and the Carlyle Hotel in New York; showrooms for Steelcase and Georg Jensen; the Kent Memorial Library and The Providence Athenaeum; schools such as Princeton Prospect Center and Wesleyan Athletic Center; Standard Brands Research Center; and the *Fantasia* and *Fiesta* passenger ships in European waters.

Warren Platner in his studio in 1963
developing a modern classic.
Photography by Joe A. Watson

"As an architect, interior designer and decorator, in creating furniture designs I consider how these products can be extensively used in many places by many people with differing tastes over a long period of time. I strive for a timeless quality."

"The 'Design' is, of course, a synthesis of function, form and fabrication."

"To have a timeless quality, a design must be comfortable, durable and economic of space and material as well as pleasing in its simplicity of line."

The Platner Collection. Designed by Warren Platner. Manufactured by The Knoll Group. Includes lounge chair, armchair, easy chair, stool, ottoman, dining table, side table, coffee tables. Frames: vertical steel wire rods welded to circular horizontal and edge-framing rods; bright nickel finish with clear lacquer protection. Bases: clear plastic extrusion ring for smooth bottom surface. Upholstery: molded fiberglass shell with foam cushion quilting. Cushions with latex core and zipper cover attached to seat with Velcro. Available in customer's own material. Tabletops: ⅜ inch thick tempered glass or marble with beveled edge (dining table available in marble only). Marble coated with transparent polyester.
Photography courtesy of The Knoll Group

Timothy deFiebre

*T*imothy deFiebre entered the field of furniture design through theater, studying technical design and production at the Yale School of Drama and the Parsons School of Design. But interior environments whether on stage or in real life all can benefit from the type of elegant line and proportion that has always interested him—plus his devotion to wood and manipulating it to create different surface textures. So no one was surprised when his various chairs started winning awards, or when he was appointed Vice President of Design and Product Development for ICF. There he is aiding in the evolution of the company, known for bringing fine European design to the U.S., into being a domestic producer of fine American design as well.

"Obviously, I want my furniture to be usable in a variety of environments, so the first use that comes to mind is how I would it in my own environment. If I can't find broad application for a piece, then I don't think others could either."

"I think the design, its fabrication, and its function are all important and all intertwined. In my mind, design has to be functional to be design, otherwise it becomes art. The fabrication determines how we get from the idea to the finished product."

The responsibility of the designer is what I term the expansion of the language of design—and hopefully the aspiration to greatness. This is not some egomaniacal attitude. It's really a setting of goals for oneself."

Layered Wood Chair. *Designed by Timothy deFiebre, 1993. Manufactured by ICF. Solid maple—natural, black-stained or custom stained—and also available with an upholstered seat. An armless stacking chair that features a seat and back made of machined ⅛ inch maple ply. The three layers of machined ply are glued together at alternating 90 degree angles to form a rigid grid pattern. The work is an exploration in creating surface texture by altering the surface of the wood.*
Photography 1993 Abby Sadin Photography, Inc.

Ronchamp Chair. *Designed by Timothy deFiebre, 1993. Manufactured by ICF. Solid maple and available with wood or upholstered seat. Finishes include natural, black-stained and custom-stained colors. Inspired by and named after the chapel in France designed by Le Corbusier. Features an organically shaped back that curves gracefully down to meet with the front legs. The curved edges of the seat and the back supports give it a softened appearance reminiscent of the roof and walls of the chapel.*
Photography 1993 Abby Sadin Photography, Inc.

Stan Taylor

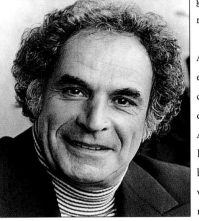

Stan Taylor, chief executive officer and design talent of E·N·T Enterprises, has played many roles in the design industry, from architect to interior designer, to designer of furniture, wall coverings, and textiles, including his award-winning woven leathers. These lush leather interlacements he and his partner Ted Nittler have put to use on two of Taylor's most recent designs, which Taylor says involve a perspective gleaned from the total of his past experience.

A native New Yorker, Taylor graduated from New York University and completed graduate work in industrial design and interior decorating at the American School of Design. Following service in the U.S. Army, he began his career as a textile designer where his talents were quickly recognized by the fashion as well as interior furnishings field. Later, moving to Southern California, he designed numerous interiors, served as consultant for motion pictures and television, and also developed a business importing antiques. Still later he developed an extensive line of European antique furniture reproductions, maintaining a wholesale showroom in Southern California as well as an office and factory in Europe.

"As an interior designer, furniture and product designer, I am immediately drawn to visualizing the finished product in a variety of settings and uses. The question I ask myself prior to committing concept to paper is: What will the skeletal shape be? Will the design have a distinctive personality? How adaptable will the form be to a variety of decorative styles and backgrounds? Is it comfortable in performing its function?"

"In my opinion, function is the primary motivation which leads to a new development. The challenge for the designer is to incorporate the function into a harmonious and pleasing shape. Added pluses are my choices and uses of distinctive materials. For example, in recent years I have adapted ecologically sound leathers into multiple designs and uses."

"The designer has the responsibility to provide sturdy, well-engineered, long-lasting construction. We must be considerate as to choices of production materials so as not to add to the depletion of natural resources. Our leathers are byproducts of food production."

Amalfi Lounge and Ottoman.
Designed by Stan Taylor, 1993. Hand-braided genuine leather. Shown without cushions to reveal leather braiding. The ottoman is not usually cushioned and doubles nicely as a side table, sometimes with a glass top. Shown in British tan; also available in chestnut, brown, black and bone. Manufactured by E·N·T (Edwin.Nittler.Taylor) Enterprises. On view in the showrooms of Jack Lenor Larsen nationwide.
Photography by Russell Einhorn

Moulay Lounge and Ottoman.
Designed by Stan Taylor, 1991. Hand-braided genuine leather. Shown without cushions to reveal leather braiding. Available in chestnut color leather, as shown, as well as British tan, black and bone. Manufactured by E·N·T (Edwin.Nittler.Taylor) Enterprises. On view in the showrooms of Jack Lenor Larsen nationwide.
Photography by Russell Einhorn

Goralnick ∗ Buchanan A&D, Inc. Barry Goralnick ◦ Michael Buchanan

Goralnick ∗ Buchanan A&D, Inc. is the pairing of architect Barry Goralnick and decorator Michael Buchanan. They have found that their individual training and perspective have made for an invigorating design synergy, enabling them to work as a seamless team...creatively.

Partners for nine years, they have developed a single voice, with both being interested in the Neo-Classical and in classic decorative motifs and in adapting these forms to pieces suited to modern function. An important element in their design is their adding to their preferred traditional styles a contemporary sense of scale and proportion.

"We began designing furniture and lighting as a response to the fact that we couldn't find many of the items we required. Having a knowledge of the market and the way other designers worked, we feel that we are able to fill a need in the market. We feel we strike a balance between interests we like to pursue in design and devising designs that other designers will choose to buy. We have already expanded to accessories and needlepoint rugs and pillows."

"Like all good design, form and function and execution are inextricable. There is a general misperception that all our time is spent on design. We spend a great deal of time perfecting the designs and making sure that the quality is always the best, and working closely with the craftsmen. Our pieces are made by hand one at a time. The quality is the finest of materials, whether bronze, steel, wood…."

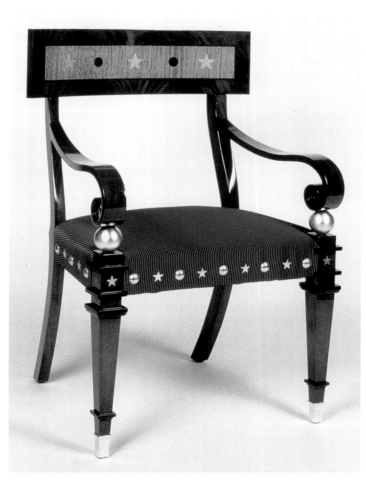

Scroll Armchair from The Endymion Series. *Designed and manufactured by Goralnick ∗ Buchanan A&D, Inc., 1992. Mahogany with ebonized detailing. Crest is crotch mahogany with ebonized stringing, inset of silkwood with inlaid brass stars and ebonized circles. Round and star-shaped upholstery tacks. Custom colors, lacquers and woods, and additional gilding available. Series includes dining table, console, bench and mirror. Photography by Steve Tague*

Bench from The Endymion Series. *Designed and manufactured by Goralnick ∗ Buchanan A&D, Inc., 1992. Mahogany with silkwood inlay. Ebonized circles. Brass stars. Custom colors, lacquers and woods available. Customer's own material, tassels and trim. Series includes dining table, console, mirror and chair. Photography by Luigi Pellettieri*

JOSÉ LUIS PÉREZ ORTEGA

A designer of many chairs being produced by Spanish companies and distributed around the world, José Luis Pérez Ortega combines the ability to answer contract furniture manufacturers' practical needs along with great style. Pieces by him, while often intended at first for the office, usually manage to find their way into the home of clients responding to his blend of aesthetics with furniture that really works.

After graduating from the Escuela de Artes y Oficios, José Luis Pérez Ortega worked on a number of interior design projects in Madrid. He

PHOTOGRAPHY COURTESY OF JOSÉ LUIS PÉREZ ORTEGA

then moved to Italy for five years, from 1977 to 1981, receiving a degree from the Polytechnic School of Design in Milan. He has worked on various architectural and industrial design projects at the Studio of Gianfranco Frattini and collaborated with the design department of the Bernini Carate Brianza Furniture Factory in Milan. Since 1981 he has been professor in Madrid's Experimental School of Design.

"While I am creating an original object, I am unconsciously placing it in its ideal space. The objects seem to take on a life of their own and develop their own trajectory during the time they are used. For me, closed spaces are intimate and I want to create an atmosphere where the objects are in harmony with their surroundings but do not sacrifice their integrity to them. For example, the chair is part of the room but it also has its own identity."

"Function is implicit. The manufacturer knows best about making the furniture. Design is the message of the designer and has a symbolic value and aesthetic form. Every form can be functional or well-made but the symbolic value is subtle and only the designer can communicate this. Ideally, the perfect combination of these three components—design, fabrication and function—creates the harmony of the piece.

"Also, objects can have a relationship among themselves. They do not have to be coordinated and can be totally different. What unites them are the feelings of the person who lives with them."

"The responsibilities of the designer can be many. While it is important to take into consideration such aspects as ecology, ergonomics and longevity, it also depends on each particular case and circumstance. I believe I have a moral and ethical responsibility to the product as well as to the client and consumer which is crucial to the outcome of the product. There are certain specific needs that the client has and I have to design the product while putting something of myself into it as well."

Sillón Frailero. *Designed by José Luis Pérez Ortega, 1987. Manufactured by Artespaña. Exterior frame finished in stainless steel or black epoxy. Interior frame of back and seat in cinched beech wood and covered with foam rubber. Upholstered in leather or fabric. Carved arm comes in two different finishes: light walnut wood or black lacquer. Photography courtesy of Artespaña*

"Once upon a time, in a country very far away called Spain, lived a king and queen so austere and discreet that they usually sat upon very uncomfortable chairs. However, they came to almost rule the world from this type of chair."

—José Luis Pérez Ortega

Sillaflorida. *Designed by José Luis Pérez Ortega, 1993. Manufactured by Artespaña. Mahogany, upholstered in velvet tufted with silk roses, legs finished in silver.*

Designed for the Spanish stand in the exposition "Progetti e Territori" in the Abitare il Tempo fair in Verona, Italy, in October 1993. It was organized by A.N.I.E.M.E. (Associacion Nacional de Industriales y Exportadores de Meubles) and was produced by Artespaña. This chair belonged to a dining room that formed part of an eclectic mixture of furniture, a new interpretation of a popular Spanish house called "Carmen." Photography courtesy of A.N.I.E.M.E.

Mark Brazier-Jones

*I*t is not surprising to find that Mark Brazier-Jones lives in an ancient farmhouse in the depths of the English countryside. Many of the forms and images he uses as the raw ingredients for his designs are drawn from ancient cultures and nature, a reflection of his interest in universal archetypes and the emotional and spiritual suggestibility of symbolic combinations.

"I have many clients from all over the world, and of those I have met it has been most interesting how they have recognized and appreciated the subliminal narratives I had unconsciously built into the work. One of my clients is an astrophysicist who has dedicated his life to the study of black holes. He told me that in his field of study many hundreds of scientists may each work a whole lifetime on a single equation only with the hope of finding the essence of the next question. This, he tells me, is the nature of the progression of science. Then, once in a while, there comes somebody

who brings the theoretical works of all these many scientists together to make a cohesive theory which is the basis of the next question to be addressed.

"This description struck tremendous resonance with me, and I visualized at once what I had been doing. I had been creating amalgams of previous cultural archetypal imagery, combined with my own aesthetic intuitions. And this, of course, was totally fitting to my age, or rather the age of my society. We are reaching the end of the twentieth century, and we are regurgitating all our past cultures. Reevaluating. Discarding. Retaining. Look at fashion and pop. As we reach the end of 1999 we are going to see a more frantic catharsis of all that has gone before it, a desperate search for what is to follow. I suppose the idea is that we will discard that which proved worthless and retain that of use.

"I intend using my craft as my vehicle of discovery to explore my true nature. Whatever it is that is considered to be my present style will metamorphose in conjunction with my personal growth."

"To design good furniture simply requires an understanding of good living, as it is with architecture or interior design."

"Different pieces have different priorities. Design is usually number one. A good piece should look well proportioned at a distance, tactile and inviting close up, comfortable and solid in use, surprising in detail."

"My responsibility is to respond truly to my instincts and to maintain a state of whimsical sincerity."

Dolphintail Chairs. *Designed and manufactured by Mark Brazier-Jones, 1990. Aluminum. Shown with a wood/glass/steel dining table which Jones designed in 1991.*
Photography courtesy of Mark Brazier-Jones

Wingback Chair. *Designed and manufactured by Mark Brazier-Jones, 1988. Bronze. Limited edition, sold out. One purchased by the Musée des Arts Decoratifs, Louvre, Paris.*
Photography courtesy of Mark Brazier-Jones

Nanna Ditzel

"*I* am educated as a furniture designer, but work in many other fields," says this Danish designer first known to many through the "legless interiors" she designed with her late husband Jørgen Ditzel. At a joint exhibition in the early 1950s at Winkel & Magnussen, they demonstrated

how one's life at home could be conducted on many different levels, through a series of platforms rather than traditional furnishings. Her ideas were new then and, for Nanna Ditzel, have remained so ever since. Her hallmark always combines her devotion to color and elegant line with a quest for relevant innovation.

"I find there is a relationship between all the items in our surroundings," says Ditzel who also designs textiles, jewelry, tableware and exhibitions.

"The important thing is to know what you want to achieve, to have a concept of your own. It is then part of the work-in-progress to coordinate techniques, functions and other demands. The final product is the responsibility of the designer from any point of view."

Folding Stool. *Designed by Nanna Ditzel, 1992. Laminated veneer, solid maple and brass fittings. Prototype. Photography by Schnakenburg & Brahl*

Bench for Two. *Designed by Nanna Ditzel, 1989. Frame: solid black lacquered maple. Seat: maple-veneered plywood. Produced by Fredericia Stolefabrik. "This design is for those who wish to spend a little while together," says Ditzel. Therefore, the front edge forms a right angle, allowing the persons to face each other.*

The back consists of 1 mm airplane plywood, veneered with maple. When the plywood is still flat, it receives a silk-screen print in the pattern of concentric black circles, the center being marked with a red dot. Then it is fixed to the seat by black screws to create a coneshape. Photography by Schnakenburg & Brahl

Two Chairs—a Butterfly.
Designed by Nanna Ditzel, 1991.
Produced by Fredericia Stolefabrik.
The chairs are identical but mirrored.
The back and seat are cut from one piece
of 2 mm fiberboard, sprayed red and silk
screen printed while still flat, then folded.
The seat is mounted to a 10 mm pre-
shaped laminated board to which the
steel frame with legs also is fixed. The
back is flexible and the chair is lightweight.
Photography by Schnakenburg & Brahl

Chair. Designed by Nanna Ditzel,
1992. Perforated airplane veneer and
compressed ash. Produced by Fredericia
Stolefabrik.
Photography by Schnakenburg & Brahl

CABINETRY

Ron Arad
Arthur de Mattos Casas
Transit Design
Antonia Astori.
Robert Garcia/Therien & Co.
Edward David Nieto
Steve Chase

Alfredo De Vido

Jaime Tresserra

Ettore Sottsass, Jr.

George J. Sowden

Coop Himmelblau

Jean-Pierre Heim

Shigeru Uchida

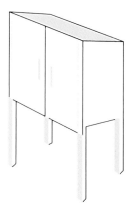

Ron Arad

R on Arad's background in art as well as in architecture has been evident throughout his work in furniture design. The creations born in his London studio are sparked by his atypical perspective of mundane objects and materials, seeing them as rich canvases rather than ordinary substances not worthy of attention. Then he beckons them to serve in ranks usually perceived as above their station. Yet this all came about without much intent other than just the chance to work.

Born in Tel Aviv, Arad studied at the Jerusalem Academy of Art before moving to London in 1973 and studying further at the Architectural Association-School of Architecture under Peter Cook and B. Tschumi.

In 1981 he founded One Off as a new format for a design practice. This meant that there was to be a workshop creating furniture and objects as an integral part of the practice. Projects could start on the drawing board or the workbench. In addition to the sophisticated sculptural steel pieces produced in the London workshop, Arad's creations have expanded to include designs for various manufacturers including Kartell, Driade, Moroso, Alessi and Vitra.

In 1989 Arad established Ron Arad Associates, initially to realize the interior architecture of the new Tel Aviv Opera. The practice is thriving, and while for Arad and his architect partner Alison Brooks the opera has been the major ongoing project (completion is scheduled for August 1994), the office has realized several commissions in London and Milan, including its own design-build project in Chalk Farm, London, for the firm's design and architectural practice.

Current projects include a studio/house for a publisher in Germany, a restaurant in London, and a fashion shop in Milan.

> *"I started designing furniture as a way out of working for other architects. As a young graduate, I wanted to work for myself and at the time no one asked me to design a concert hall or even a private house. Furniture was something I could design and make on my own."*

> *"You cannot make rules," he says. "Different criteria apply to different pieces of design. Sometimes it's the fabrication, other times it's the performance, the cost, the weight, the color...."*

> *"The designer's responsibility? None. To be a good citizen. The rest will be taken care of by history."*

This Mortal Coil.
Designed by Ron Arad, 1993.
Freestanding bookshelves of blackened
tempered steel strip coiled to form a spiral.
The form is retained by partitions
through riveted hinges. The hinges allow
the coil to move in a spring action.
Photography by Christoph Kicherer

Industrial Bookworm. Designed by
Ron Arad, 1993. Wall-mounted book-
shelves in stainless sprung steel. The form
is retained by winged, hinged brackets.
The form varies with each installation.
Photography by Erica Calvi

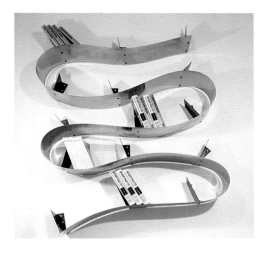

One Way or Another.
Designed by Ron Arad, 1993.
Blackened tempered steel strip, the form
retained by hinged partitions. The overall shape becomes distorted with the
weight of books.
Photography by Erica Calvi

Bookworm. Designed by Ron Arad,
1993. Wall-mounted bookshelves in
blackened strip tempered steel. The form
is retained by "fake books" or box brackets. Size is unlimited and the form varies
with each installation.
Photography by Christoph Kicherer

117

Arthur de Mattos Casas

*D*evoted as much to the art of craftsmanship and delicate detailing as he is to essential, rational and basic design, Brazil's Arthur de Mattos Casas brings a distinctive poetry to the architecture, interior design and furniture design with which he is involved. And his involvement is broad—including the establishment of his own special store of furniture design, Casas Edições de Design, where not only his own furniture designs but also those of such other contemporary masters as Mario Botta and Giandomenico Belotti hold court. Indeed, he is the exclusive representative of their designs manufactured by the Italian company ALIAS for all of Latin America.

With a degree in Architecture and Urbanism from Mackenzie University in São Paulo in 1983, Casas has designed the architecture and interiors for more than one hundred residential, corporate, public space and hospitality projects. His work has been exhibited in Europe, the United States and Latin America. In 1989 he received the Design Award from the Museum of The Brazilian House, São Paulo.

"The three themes—architecture, interior design and furniture design—are intimately related. I always search for a contemporary language, reflecting the historic moment I am going through in the three activities in which I am working."

"When I am creating a piece of furniture, my basis is always the beauty and originality of the design, ease of production and user practicality. There isn't for me one item more important than the other."

"Besides the preoccupation with the use of the furniture, the foremost responsibility of the designer is to interpret the language, its contemporary interpretation, even if its relation comes from other historic moments. We live in the end of the twentieth century. It is the moment to reevaluate, to reread."

Africa Bar-Horizontal. *Designed by Arthur de Mattos Casas, 1992. Manufactured and distributed by Casas Edições de Design LTDA. Mahogany covered with Fresno (Australian veneer) and ebonized wood. Photography by Tuca Reinés*

Africa Bar-Vertical. *Designed by Arthur de Mattos Casas, 1992. Manufactured and distributed by Casas Edições de Design LTDA. Mahogany covered with Fresno (Australian veneer), and ebonized wood.*
Photography by Tuca Reinés

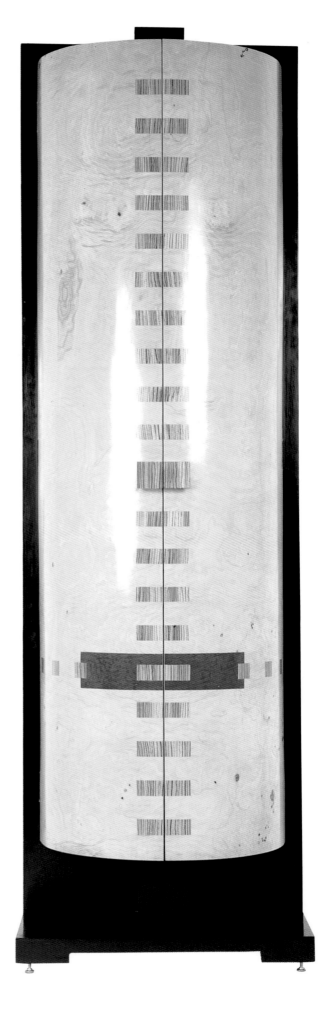

Transit Design   Giovanni Ascarelli ◦ Maurizio Macciocchi ◦ Evaristo Nicolao ◦ Danilo Parisio

*T*he aim of Studio Transit Design is to produce global architectural works, with no distinction between the architecture and the interior design, with no boundaries between art and design. To its founders, designing furniture means thinking about it from the moment the entire project starts.

Transit Design S.r.l. avails itself of the collaboration of fully qualified architects and engineers and, in particular, of the continuing advice and leadership of the firm's founders—Giovanni Ascarelli, Maurizio Macciocchi, Evaristo Nicolao and Danilo Parisio. The company is situated in Rome and has been operating in the sector of public utility infrastructures for more than twenty years. Projects completed by the firm include those in the areas of public transport, architecture for leisure, industrial buildings, office buildings, residential buildings, commercial buildings, school buildings, town-planning and landscape. It has also been responsible for the design of many products. These include the fixtures and fittings

and system of signs for the "A" line of the Rome Subway system which went into operation in 1980; numerous projects for a series of objects and furniture for public and private clients; and, in 1981, Metro-Information—a new information system allowing subway users to direct themselves clearly toward the services, the places of historic interest and the monuments of Rome.

"As architects and not interior or furniture designers, we consider the object to be put in a space is part of a 'oneness,' meaning that the project's architectural language is used time and again in objects which the client needs and which themselves transform the architectural language in relation to that space. In our projects, there is no break between the architecture of the place and its furniture; they meld together to generate a product in which our style and ideology are always recognizable. Sometimes we are urged to be especially creative and in this way objects are born breaking all traditional schemes and are the direct consequence of our contemporary culture and sensibility."

"There is no difference in purposes between furniture design and the architectural project. So in our opinion function, fabrication and design are strictly related and cannot be divided from the final result of the product."

"As architects we think longevity is the most important responsibility for a project designer, not in terms of the life duration of the object but in terms of historical and cultural meaning of the architectural symbol and its suitability within the concept of our initial project choice."

Totem. *Designed by Transit Design, 1986. Container/sculpture for sound system: wood and plastic laminate. Photography by Janos Grapow*

Paravento. Designed by Transit Design, 1984-88. Container/sculpture: painted wood.
Photography by Giovanna Piemonti

Totem. Designed by Transit Design, 1983. Sculpture cupboards: wood and plastic laminate.
Photography by Giovanna Piemonti

Parallelepipedi. Designed by Transit Design, 1983. Sculpture wardrobe: wood and plastic laminate.
Photography by Giovanna Piemonti

Antonia Astori

Milanese designer Antonia Astori began her association with the manufacturer Driade in 1968, contributing her research in systems furniture through various lines of modular furniture that enables the user to personally interpret how the parts should be combined. The Oikos system provides a uniform solution for all the problems of containing which may arise in a home, from a single piece of furniture to a complete wall system.

"The idea originated in 1973 from the prefabricated panels used in the building trade," says Astori. "It can be seen as an architectural structure for joining or separating interior spaces. The choice was therefore in favor of basic elements characterized by the greatest simplicity and by carefully studied modulation, with the abolition of all the unnecessary cluttered

detail which more often than not characterized the fully fitted walls of two decades ago."

Along with her activity in product design, Astori also is involved with interior architecture. In 1984 she began her cooperation with the French stylists Marithé and François Girbaud by designing the Parisian shop which was then followed by many others in France, Brussels, Montreal, San Francisco and Milan. In 1987 she designed the Driade office/showroom beside the factory in Caorso. She has also been involved with redesigning the interiors of the Driade-Ambiente showroom in Tokyo and the Bang & Olufsen center in Munich.

"Some designers develop their ideas first in theory and then develop the project. Others start from real facts and situations in order to verify the project itself. I belong to this second group of designers. Therefore it is my work as interior architect that determines my design of system product lines. Almost all my designs have originated from specific tasks, and then they have been industrially developed."

"A few fine arts critics assert that form and contents coincide in the arts. As far as industrial design is concerned, it is possible to say that form, function and production define together the meaning of design."

"'Good design' should take into consideration many needs—ergonomics, ecology and longevity....I believe that in the future the ecological factor will be more carefully investigated, for it now is a relatively new aspect of both our education and project experience."

Oikos. *Designed by Antonia Astori, 1973. Manufactured by Driade. Structures: wood-based composition panels finished with white melamine or smooth metallized gray (gianostal). Fronts: wood-based composition panels finished with white melamine, ribbed smooth metallized gray (gianostal), or polyurethane paint (available in ten lacquer colors, four glossy metallic paints, or bronze, copper or aluminum embossed metallic paint). Door fronts also available with aluminum tube panel and the plugging surface in: perforated aluminum sheet, ruled aluminum with natural anodized finish, transparent glass with dark gray silk-screened perimetrical border, or satinized glass with light gray silk-screened perimetrical border. Handles: chromed steel tube, or turned brass cylinder. Plinths and continuous frontage panels are made of extruded anodized natural ribbed aluminum. In the modular version, the frontage panels are also available in smooth lacquer or varnished aluminum. Transparent walls available as fixed or door panels, consist of dark gray epoxy-color finished extruded aluminum panels, layered glass, and satinized chrome-plated brass/cylinder lock handles. Doors: hollow core available with lacquer or paint finishes and of an extruded aluminum jamb, with flared profile, available with the same finishes; satinized chrome-plated brass handle and lock.*

Robert Garcia/Therien & Co.

*R*obert Garcia, a native of San Francisco, first came into contact with the design field when he attended the Rudolph Schaeffer School of Design in San Francisco. The school specialized in establishing an overall design foundation with emphasis on color.

Upon graduation his first position was as a draftsman for the San Francisco architectural firm of Whisler-Patri. Within a year a position of furniture draftsman opened up in the design studio of Gump's San Francisco, headed by Eleanor M. Forbes. After five years as design assistant and designer with Gump's, he returned to architectural interiors at Whisler-Patri.

Again exploring design potential, he left San Francisco for New York where he worked for McMillen Inc. in the office of Mark Hampton.

In 1979, Garcia and another partner founded Therien & Co. Inc. in San Francisco, and later opened a Los Angeles office and showroom, specializing in antiques and custom design furniture.

"As an interior designer, I conceptualize furniture not only for its function but also for its potential to evoke an emotional response, whether in a classic spirit or by pure decorative device."

"It seems the order of design, fabrication, followed by function states my priorities in furniture design."

"The designer's responsibility certainly involves ergonomics, ecology, longevity, et cetera, as any truly successful piece of furniture must now take all currently valid concerns into consideration."

Dolphin Commode. *Designed by Robert Garcia, 1992. Veneered in lacewood. Inset Verde San Remo marble top over Greek key frieze. Incorporating single long drawer and two additional long drawers with ribbed panel, front flanked by canted pilasters continuing as block feet with serpent feet. Inspired by Catherine the Great and the Neoclassic period in Russia. Photography courtesy of Therien & Co.*

Anthemion Commode. *Designed by Robert Garcia, 1991. Karelian birch. Black granite top. Ebonized and aged gilt detail. Fitted with two drawers and gilt mounts. Inspired by Scandinavia of the Neoclassic period. Photography courtesy of Therien & Co.*

Edward David Nieto

*T*his award-winning South Florida interior designer has now launched his own furniture line, The Sō - Bē Collection, with its distinguished use of fine materials now on view in showrooms in New York, Chicago, Los Angeles and Miami.

Completing his education in 1980 with a Bachelor's degree from Temple University, Nieto's talent was recognized early in his career and he became the director of Burdines Interior Design Studio in 1985. In 1987 he became the director of corporate and residential design of Bloomingdale's in Miami. He then opened his own offices in 1991, introducing Edward David Nieto Design Group, also in Miami.

"Being exposed to the interior design industry and the availability within the industry, I felt a void for my clients' needs. I pursued creating my own design to fill the demand for unique furniture pieces that fit the realm of architectural and lifestyle efficiency. I feel that the void is being filled with my new collection."

"If the design or its fabrication or its function falls short, the other components will not work either. A good design without function is non-utilitarian, and a functional design without style is mundane. It had been my theory that form follows function follows style. I take great pride in the construction of each item in my collection, whether it is a cabinet with intricate marquetry or an upholstered chair in which the construction, although unseen, must be the best possible. I insist on the craftsmanship meeting the highest of standards."

"Regarding the designer's responsibility, I feel all furniture should be conducive to the natural comfort of one's body without sacrificing style. Also, my commitment to the environment is reflected in my use of environmentally safe products in all fabrication processes. Finally, I believe in longevity. My pieces are constructed so they might be heirlooms."

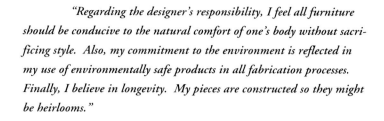

Waldorf Cabinet. *Designed by Edward David Nieto, 1993. Manufactured by Edward David Nieto Design Group. Zimbabwe granite and anigre; Madagascar ebony legs with aluminum tips; bronze pulls. Available in various wood combinations, satin or high-gloss finish. Tops available in various granites as well as inlaid woods. All specifications must be approved by Edward David Nieto to assure aesthetic beauty of cabinet.*
Photography by Peter Morpurgo

Savoy Cabinet. *Designed by Edward David Nieto, 1992. Manufactured by Edward David Nieto Design Group and Sivyer Steel Corp. Anigre and Madagascar ebony with cast aluminum legs and pulls. Available in various wood combinations, satin of high-gloss finish, all hand inlays, customized interior.*
Photography by Peter Morpurgo

Steve Chase

Steve Chase founded his namesake design firm, located in Rancho Mirage, California, in 1980 following a lengthy and noted affiliation with Arthur Elrod Associates of Palm Springs. The international clientele list of Steve Chase Associates includes entertainment and business leaders.

Chase has been the recipient of many professional honors, including being named to *Interior Design* magazine's Hall of Fame award, and Designer of the Year presented to him by *Designers West* magazine.

Chase's intense interest in art has generated a significant collection of contemporary art, displayed in his private residences and Rancho Mirage office. Recent additions to his collection include painters of the California Plein Air School. While his collection contains museum quality works, he constantly acknowledges and seeks out work by young and upcoming artists. Contributions from his collection have been made to the Palm Springs Desert Museum. Other philanthropic works include long-term support of the Living Desert Reserve, Palm Desert's renowned botanical and wildlife reserve.

"Since I have a strong architectural 'taste' anyway, and have typically designed a number of custom pieces for my projects, it seemed only a natural extension to create my own lines of furniture."

"All three—design, fabrication and function—must be successful in order for a piece to be successful. The design is not an end. Fabrication is close to an end, and its function is about as close to an end as you can get. All three must be accomplished equally well. Fabrication is in some ways the most complex. Pieces must be designed to ship and arrive in one piece."

"I would not knowingly cut down a rare tree to build a cabinet. I would not use toxic paints. If a piece isn't comfortable, it wouldn't be part of my design. Remember, most of my designs are variations on motifs I've seen in my travels around the world, and have a designed-in longevity."

Zanzibar Armoire

Marrakech Armoire

Voyager Collection. *Designed by Steve Chase, 1991. Styles and pieces include: Zanzibar (armoire, chest, headboard, desk, mirror); Marrakech (armoire, chest, headboard); Montana (armoire, chest); Cheyenne (armoire, chest); Mendocino (armoire, chest); Mandalay (armoire, chest); and Sardinia (occasional table). Various woods, colors and finishes. Manufactured by Mueller Turner. Available through Mimi London.*

Photography :
(page 126) by Arthur Coleman
(page 127) courtesy of Mueller Turner

Cheyenne Armoire

Mendocino Armoire

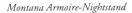

Montana Armoire-Nightstand

Alfredo De Vido

*T*hroughout the years that New York architect Alfredo De Vido has been involved with large scale projects, he has been creating every aspect of residential interiors as well. The furniture, one-of-a-kind pieces designed for specific clients and specific spaces, reflects his emphasis throughout his architectural works, his books and his lectures—the importance of totally unified design.

De Vido's professional training includes a Bachelor of Architecture degree from Carnegie-Mellon University, a Master of Fine Arts from Princeton University, and a Diploma in Town Planning from the Royal Academy of Fine Arts, Copenhagen. Awards during his years of study have since been followed by many from national, state and city organizations.

He is also the author of two books, *Designing Your Client's House—An Architect's Guide to Meeting Design Goals and Budgets*, and *Innovative Management Techniques for Architectural Design and Construction* published in 1983 and 1984 by the Whitney Library of Design.

"Architects understand how the furniture should fit into the space of the room or house."

"In furniture design, the design is probably most important, but function (comfort) is especially so also."

"The designer's responsibility? Ergonomics and longevity."

Storage unit for the Quinones/Bieganek residence, *East Hampton, New York. Designed by Alfredo De Vido, 1991. Fabricated by Ray McCarthy, Sag Harbor Furniture. Ash and walnut. Photography © by Norman McGrath*

Furniture for the Richard Walderman residence, *New York, New York. Designed by Alfredo De Vido, 1993. Fabricated by Ray McCarthy, Sag Harbor Furniture. Includes: End table of ash and walnut; eight drawer chest of ash, walnut and cherry; and a bookcase of ash and walnut. Photography ©1993 by Norman McGrath*

Jaime Tresserra

ombining a richly varied career in the decorative arts, from jewelry design to the rehabilitation of numerous Catalan country houses, Jaime Tresserra brings to his furniture design a commitment to combining fine handicraft and the most noble of materials. For his furniture, produced by J. Tresserra Design, Barcelona, the material primarily used is walnut veneer, finished with various light and dark toned varnishes and blended with inlaid marquetry.

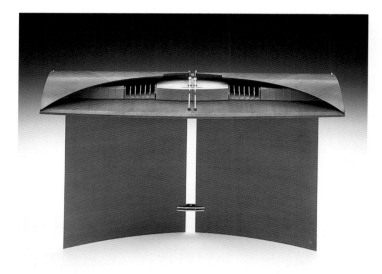

Tresserra's work has been featured in numerous exhibitions including two in New York in 1989: "Catalonia Design" organized by the Generalitat de Catalunya; and "Barcelona/The Emerging Design" organized by Japan Air Lines. His work also appeared in "Les Capitales Européens du Nouveau Design" organized by Centre Georges Pompidou, Paris. In 1990 Tresserra received the International Design Review Award from International Design Editions New York, and from the same organization received the 1992 Golden Award for his Attaché Dune.

Carlton-House Butterfly. *Designed by Jaime Tresserra, 1988. Walnut wood. Interior in sycamore. Natural varnish finish. Iron fittings: nickel-plated, with leather tone details. Photography by Globus*

"When I design a piece of furniture, I cannot exclude it from a definite space with a definite light, and from the specific people living in it…whom I keep in mind always."

"The design is the poetry. Its function…the servitude. And the fabrication…the drama."

"When one speaks of the designer's responsibility, it is impossible to separate the concepts of ergonomics, ecology, and longevity. The just measurement is the key. Example: some extra minutes of life of a disposable paper cup, after having used it, would be the equivalent in efficacy and longevity to one hundred years of useful life in a piece of furniture."

Secreter Carpett. *Designed by Jaime Tresserra, 1987. Available through J. Tresserra Design. Walnut wood secretary. Varnish finish: light/dark. Interior in sycamore. Iron fittings: silver-plated with pekary straps. Photography by Globus*

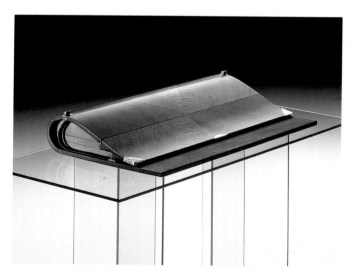

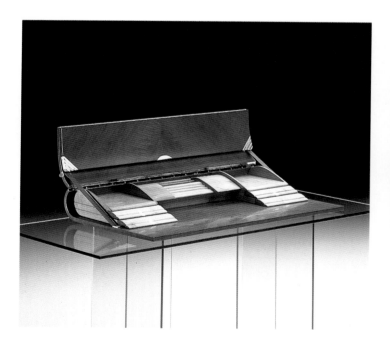

Samuro. Designed by Jaime Tresserra,
1989. Available through J. Tresserra
Design. Double body chest of drawers in
walnut wood. Natural varnish finish.
Iron fittings: leather tone.
Photography by Globus

Ettore Sottsass, Jr.

Architect/designer Ettore Sottsass, Jr. was born in 1917 in Innsbruck, Austria. He graduated from the polytechnic University of Turin in 1939, and in 1947 he started his own architecture and design studio in Milan, participating in architectural competitions and designing various residential buildings, hotels, and schools. He has been a collaborator on numerous Triennales and has had numerous individual and group shows in Italy and abroad.

He is internationally known as one of the initiators of the renewal of design and architecture that went beyond the restrictive functionalism of the years prior to and following World War II. His work has concentrated particularly on attempts to find ways, above all sensorial, to define forms as well as spaces for domestic life. He has given color great importance as a source of potential energy and a symbol of vitality in contrast to the rigid intellectualism of structures.

In 1980 he founded Sottsass Associati together with four young designers, continuing his activity as designer and architect. The following year he started "Memphis" in collaboration with friends and young architects, which shortly became an almost mythical symbol of "New Design."

"The communications jumble of the contemporary marketplace, where everyone is both a consumer and a producer of messages, raises a challenge that every professional must meet: the attainment of the highest level of consciousness in the manipulation of the technical tools of a job, to control these tools, and use them to communicate in a meaningful and sophisticated way."

"Design, in its broadest sense, encompasses engineering, compatibility of product and market, and image manipulation. Because of the growing sophistication of the market and the emphasis on communication through image, the role of design in helping define the expression of culture and technology has increased dramatically in the past few decades. The designer must bridge two worlds: merchandising, which requires innovative but salable goods, and engineering, which generates sophisticated technology. Between these poles, design must take into account sociological changes, cultural trends, and philosophical evolution in its attempt to give form to a product. Utilized as a basic component of any project, design can ensure added value and offer better placement in the market. Design innovation enables business to exercise its intuition and ingenuity to improve engineering and tackle new markets."

"Modern society, as a network of cultural phenomena, provides the points of departure for design investigations. Ours is a society of instant communication, fluid markets and global awareness. It is violent/peace loving, international/nationalistic, dogmatic/uncertain, but essentially collagist, in search of alternatives, always with the goal of improving the quality of life. While different approaches and strategies are employed from Japan to Italy, from India to California, people's hopes and dreams, problems and illusions, find expression in the architecture they build and the products they consume."

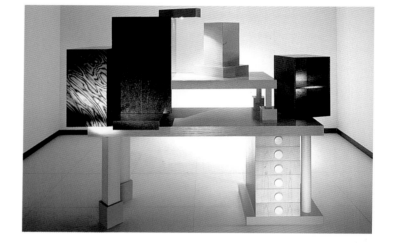

Just Back from New Guinea.
Designed by Ettore Sottsass, 1987.
Various wood veneers. Fabricated by
Renzo Brugola-Lissone. Limited production. Contact: Sottsass Associati.
Photography courtesy of Sottsass Associati

Red Forest. Designed by Ettore Sottsass, 1992. Lacquered wood and removable shelves in extra light glass. Fabricated by Marelli and Taglibue. Limited production. Contact: Sottsass Associati. Photography courtesy of Sottsass Associati

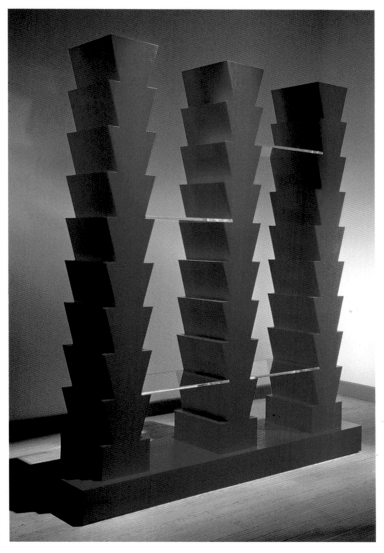

We Went to Crete. Designed by Ettore Sottsass, 1987. Various wood veneers and marble. Fabricated by Renzo Brugola-Lissone. Limited production. Contact: Sottsass Associati. Photography courtesy of Sottsass Associati

Carlton. Designed by Ettore Sottsass, 1987. Plastic laminate veneer. Available through Memphis. Photography courtesy of Sottsass Associati

George J. Sowden

"ew design no longer works for the nonexistent standardized majority, but pushes on with its youthful, individualistic energy…constantly changing, creating and feeding the communications networks." George J. Sowden's commentaries about design are as richly provocative as are his designs.

Relocated from London to Milan since 1970 when he commenced a long collaboration as consultant for Olivetti, Sowden has worked on projects of the utmost currency, from Olivetti's first computers to its most recent ink jet printers, electronic organizers and PC-based typewriters. During the same twenty years he has built up a personal decorative language as well, creating a long series of works which he refers to as Design Research.

These research works (drawings, models, prototypes and installations in exhibition), enabled him to become, in 1981, a founding member of the Memphis design movement, for which he designed numerous pieces of furniture, objects and textiles.

Sowden recently designed a collection of furniture for MK Shizuoka in Japan. In 1990 he prepared an exhibition of architectural drawings in Tokyo, and in 1990–91 a traveling exhibition of his work was presented by the Musées des Arts Decoratifs in Bordeaux, Marseilles and Lyon.

"The communication of the work is the most important…and anyway, if by design I can speak, it's up to me to decide if I want to shout or whisper."

"Everything around us is manmade. The designer has a very large share of the responsibility."

"New design has now become part of global mass-media communication which presupposes a simultaneous use of diversified images, codes and visual languages. In spite of their intolerance to each other these manage to be transmitted over the whole planet and appreciated not because of any similarity but because of their diversity. The strength with which any single image or message stimulates our senses, minds or dreams establishes its success and measures its beauty. We are now using subjective, objective, emotional and intellectual messages in colorful composition. We no longer need to ask ourselves what is the right style or what is good taste. The problem has been wiped out with a single blow—we do not even raise the question!"

d'Antibe Cabinet. *Designed by George J. Sowden, 1981. Painted wood/silk-screened decoration. In production by Memphis.*
Photography by Studio Azzurro

The Red, Yellow, Blue, Green and Purple Tallboy. Designed by George J. Sowden, 1990. Produced by The Gallery, The Netherlands. Painted wood. Manufactured to order.
Photography by Ilvio Gallo

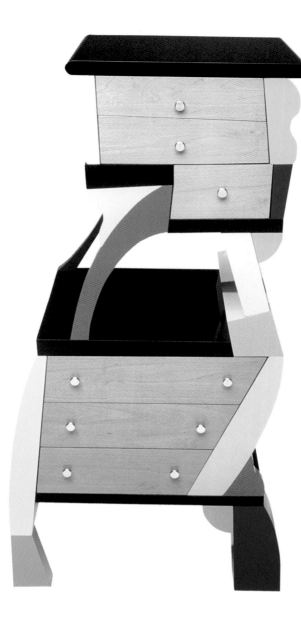

G 2 Tallboy. Designed by George J. Sowden, 1988. Produced by MK MAEDA Shizuoka. Painted wood. Limited production.
Photography by Takairo Inoue

George Cabinet. Designed by George J. Sowden, 1987. Painted wood/decorated plastic laminate. Limited production by Memphis.
Photography by Santi Caleca

Coop Himmelblau Wolf D. Prix ◦ Frank Stepper ◦ Helmut Swiczinsky

"*A*s you know, architecture needs at least three supports in order to stand firm," says Wolf D. Prix. "We noticed that in our last few projects we had started questioning the third support. What we were interested in was movement. Thus, we designed a mobile kitchen with adjustable tables and swinging or pull-out parts."

Revolutionary has been a constant attribute of the work of Coop Himmelblau, founded by Prix and Helmut Swiczinsky in 1968 in Vienna, Austria. With a second office in Los Angeles managed by partner Frank Stepper, their projects have been situated in the United States and Japan as

PHOTOGRAPHY ©VITLIA KIRCHNER

well as in Europe, and their work has been exhibited at the Museum of Modern Art, New York, and at the Centre Georges Pompidou in Paris. Throughout, Coop Himmelblau has become known for its deconstructivist direction exemplified by the X-Time Kitchen System.

With the mobile EWE kitchen, the user need never be hemmed in by stationary walls. The designers, who began designing kitchens for EWE in 1974, made sure all its parts could be adapted to the user's needs rather than pre-existing architectural geometries. A multi-functional assemblage of work surfaces, minibar, storage box, sink, dishwasher and stovetop are all movable about their stainless-steel column and beam support. In addition, the wheel-mounted electric oven can be used as a serving cart, keeping food warm and easily accessible. Also, the ironing-board-countertop can be adjusted electronically to any height.

"The chair is a house. The house is a city. The city is a chair."

"Design-Fab-Func is the new term for furniture design because it expresses the simultaneity of systems."

"Since architecture will be the art of the next century, the responsibility of the designer therefore will be the attitude."

The X-Time Movable Kitchen System, known in Europe as Mal-Zeit Kitchen. Designed by Coop Himmelblau's Wolf D. Prix and Helmut Swiczinsky, 1990. Manufactured by EWE-Küchen. Satin-finished, painted and perforated sheet-steel, tubular steel, solid wood, green and mirrored glass, sandblasted Plexiglas, Corian. Photography by Josef Hoflehner

Jean-Pierre Heim

*T*o Jean-Pierre Heim, whose much awarded architecture practice has grown into a multi-disciplinary organization providing its international clientele with every aspect of design service, it only seemed natural to launch Design Connection International. A subsidiary of Jean-Pierre Heim & Associates in Paris and New York, this company handles graphic design, packaging, retail and furniture design. It also only seemed natural to Mr. Heim that much of the furniture he designs should be stylistically influenced by the discipline in which he first started.

When Le Pavillon Bastille opened in Paris in 1991, Jean-Pierre Heim transfixed the hospitality industry with his thoroughly refreshing mix of musical motifs combined with architectural ones—in homage not only to the hotel's location, near the new Paris opera house, but also to the nineteenth century building's past. Today clients are finding that Le Pavillon Bastille's furnishings, which particularly in the guest rooms make the most of limited space, add to the spacious feeling—even as they convey a monumental presence—in their homes as well.

"I am an architect. To me, the most important aspect of furniture design is the design itself. The designer's primary responsibility is to create a piece that pleases someone aesthetically."

Los Angeles *from Pavillon line. Designed by Jean-Pierre Heim, 1991. Manufactured by Design Connection International. A multipurpose piece that combines mini-fridge, closet, television stand, mirror and vase. Photography by Arcadia*

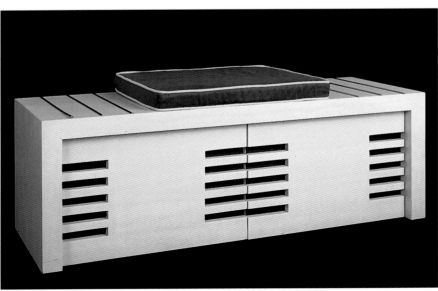

Paris *from Pavillon line. Jean-Pierre Heim, 1991. Manufactured by Design Connection International. Desk/filing cabinet. Photography by Philip Heying*

New York from Pavillon line.
Designed by Jean-Pierre Heim, 1991.
Manufactured by Design Connection
International. Combines clock, light,
television, a closet with drawers and
hanging space on either side.
Photography by Philip Heying

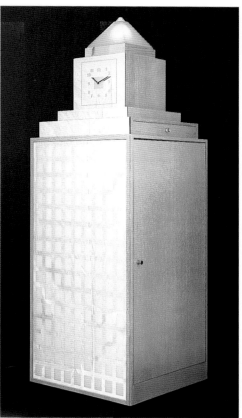

Shigeru Uchida

*D*ecisive, innovative and spare throughout all his design, from the smallest accessory to an entire residence, it is not surprising to hear Shigeru Uchida say his approach to interior and furniture design is the same. "They both belong to the same order," says Uchida who established the Tokyo design firm Studio 80 with Toru Nishioka in 1981.

Uchida graduated from the Kuwasawa Design School in Tokyo where he has served as lecturer ever since. He has also lectured at Tokyo University of Art & Design, Domus Academy in Milan, and at Columbia University, Washington State University and Parsons School of Design in the United States. Examples showing the variety of his work during the past decade are the Wave Building in Roppongi, Tokyo (1983); The World Design Expo '89 YATAI in Nagoya (1989); and the Dear Vera clock introduced by Alessi in 1991. His furniture designs are in the permanent collections of the Metropolitan Museum of Art in New York, the San Francisco Museum of Art, and the Montreal Museum of Decorative Arts.

"Designing interiors and furniture are acts as natural to me as cooking in daily life. My interiors can be realized through the placement of furniture or objects. At the same time, my furniture is a part of the interior. Hence, my perspective is impartial regarding these two areas of design."

"It is difficult to state whether the design itself, or its fabrication, or its function is most important in furniture design. They are all important. However, the relationship between the space and furniture is more important for my design."

"I believe that my main theme for design is to give great consideration to mankind and ecology. It is inevitable that we are causing some kind of devastation to nature as long as we are making things. Hence, I would like to create furniture and things with true value which are not wasteful. When I design, I try to make things or spaces that last for a long time, which would prevent the immediate waste. We should always be aware that we designers and architects are highly responsible for what we realize in society."

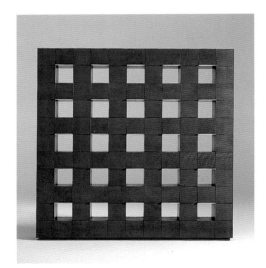

Chest of Drawers *KAGU 1991. Designed by Shigeru Uchida/Studio 80 for the 1991 exhibition of his work entitled KAGU. Manufactured by Chairs. Cherry with C.L. finish and steel with baked melamine finish. Photography by Nacása & Partners Inc.*

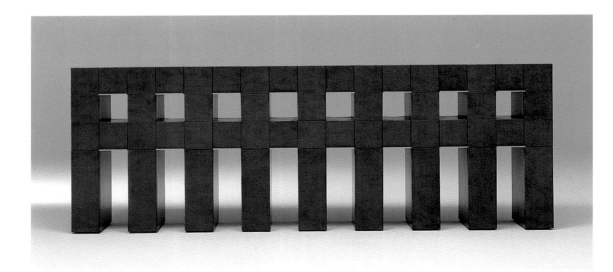

Sideboard *KAGU 1991. Designed by Shigeru Uchida/Studio 80, 1991. Manufactured by Chairs. Cherry with C.L. finish and steel with baked melamine finish. Photography by Nacása & Partners Inc.*

Chest of Drawers x 2 *KAGU 1991 .*
Designed by Shigeru Uchida/Studio 80,
1991. Manufactured by UMS Pastoe
B.V. Bubinga, Tamo veneer with wax
finish.
Photography by Nacása & Partners Inc.

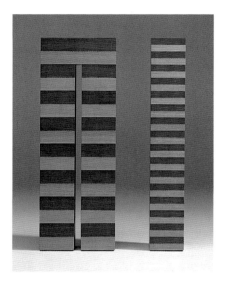

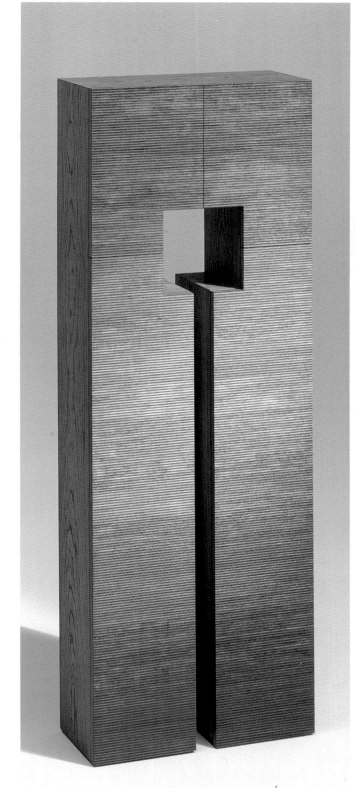

Shelf *KAGU 1991 . Designed by*
Shigeru Uchida/Studio 80, 1991.
Manufactured by UMS Pastoe B. V.
Bubinga, Tamo veneer with wax finish.
Photography by Nacása & Partners Inc.

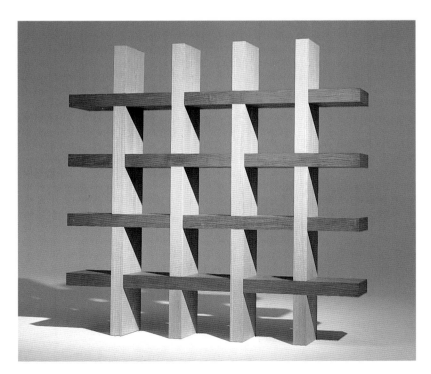

Cabinet *KAGU 1991. Designed by*
Shigeru Uchida/Studio 80, 1991.
Manufactured by UMS Pastoe B.V.
Bubinga veneer with wax finish.
Photography by Nacása & Partners Inc.

UPHOLSTERED PIECES

Goodman Charlton

John Hutton

Michael Wolk

Afra and Tobia Scarpa

Sandra Nunnerly

Milo Baughman

Noel Jeffrey

Adam Tihany

Toshiyuki Kita

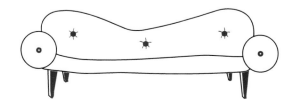

UPHOLSTERED PIECES

Ronn Jaffe
Shepard Vineburg
Michael Graves
Charles A. Reimann
Robert Stuffings
Lauren Rottet
Larry Totah
Harry Segil
Ergo Design Works
Peter Shelton and Lee F. Mindel

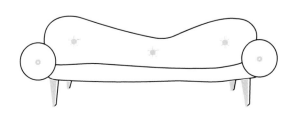

Goodman Charlton   Jeffrey Goodman · Steven Charlton

*F*urniture/interior designers Jeffrey Goodman and Steven Charlton always had a passion for the glamour and scale of the California lifestyle and, since their business had grown beyond their space and manufacturing capabilities in New York, they decided to move to Los Angeles in 1987. Yet however much the romance and sensuality of their designs purposefully refer to various periods, these two partners don't think of their look as retrouvé but as completely modern.

They recently completed the extensive renovation of the 14,000 square foot recording facilities for The Larrabee Sound Studios, which also involved designing highly individualized private lounges for Larrabee's clientele which includes Michael Jackson, Paula Abdul and Prince. More

PHOTOGRAPHY COURTESY OF GOODMAN CHARLTON

recently the designers have been concentrating on furniture design and production, and have been working closely with The Limited Stores in developing new pieces for the firm's many divisions.

Goodman *(right)* received a Bachelor of Arts degree in Visual and Environmental Studies from Harvard University in 1979. Charlton *(left)* received a Bachelor of Arts degree in Visual Communication from Brighton University, England, in 1983.

"The designer's responsibility is to provide a quality product that looks great and functions well for a long time. In our case, we feel responsible to push the 'boundaries' of design and create pieces that have not been seen before. We feel it is the designer's responsibility to be original and not just copy or imitate what has already been done."

"We approach designing furniture as 'furniture designers' not as interior designers. Our furniture designing and manufacturing capabilities greatly influence our interior design perspectives as they allow us a seemingly unlimited range in creating a room."

"The design itself, its fabrication and its function are equally important. Without these three elements working together, we could not create a successful piece of furniture. As designers we are extremely aware of comfort, durability, and style. When we start the design process for each piece, we start with the 'look,' but ultimately all the design decisions hinge on how well the piece can be built and how well it will function."

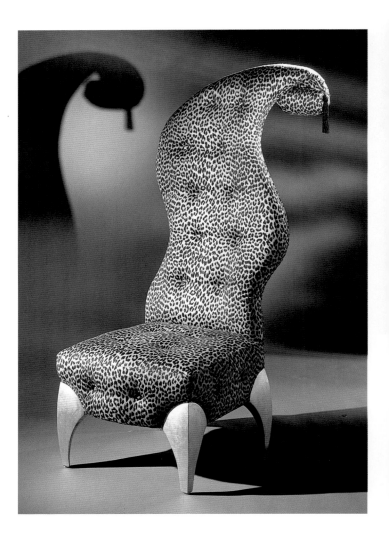

Crawford. *Designed by Goodman Charlton, 1990. Manufactured by Goodman Charlton. Photography by Amedeo Buhler*

Grande Escargot. *Designed by Goodman Charlton, 1991. Manufactured by Goodman Charlton. Photography by Amedeo Buhler*

Diabolique Sofa with Ulu Tables at
the Modern Living showroom, Los
Angeles. Designed by Goodman
Charlton, 1992. Manufactured by
Goodman Charlton.
Photography by Marvin Rand

Madame X. Designed by Goodman
Charlton, 1991. Manufactured by
Goodman Charlton.
Photography by Amedeo Buhler

Cherchez la Chaise. Designed by
Goodman Charlton, 1991.
Manufactured by Goodman Charlton.
Photography by Amedeo Buhler

John Hutton

*J*ohn Hutton proves himself master of comfort and dramatic form time and time again. As design director of the Donghia Furniture Company in New York, Hutton has created the freewheeling, high-spirited, and extraordinarily comfortable furniture for which the company is known.

Hutton, who graduated from the Fashion Institute of Technology in New York City in 1968, joined Donghia in 1978 to help Angelo Donghia, the company founder, create a furniture collection worthy of showing off the show-stopping elegance of the Donghia Textile Collection. Since that time his designs for Donghia have received many awards, and his projects applauded, the latter including the lavish Henri Bendel department store on Fifth Avenue, New York City; the furnishings for the Rainbow Room in New York City, the S.S. *Norway*, and the American Center in Paris; and

his projects for the Paris Museum Association.

"I want to take over the world by design," said Hutton when Donghia Furniture opened in Paris and other cities throughout Europe.

Hutton has received more than four commendations issued by the Roscoe Awards for outstanding furniture design. His Anziano Chair is part of the contemporary design collection at the Brooklyn Museum as well as part of the Houston Museum of Fine Arts' collection of decorative arts key to the 1980s.

"Being trained as an interior designer has given me an overall perspective of furniture, how it fits into a room and how it will be used. The pieces I design go with many other styles, from primitive to eighteenth-century French to Italian Industrial."

"Although the design and its fabrication are both important, the most important part of furniture design is, of course, its purpose or function, which to me is comfort. Comfort means more than the ability of sitting or lying down correctly. Although this is very important, comfort also means convenience, safety, practicality and appropriateness."

"The responsibility of a furniture designer today is to close the gap between waste and want. People have a need and a desire to be comfortable. I fill that need intelligently by working with the human structure and by creating products that last. I believe that by approaching furniture design intelligently one creates classics. I approach this by taking into consideration comfort, durability and environmental developments, and also by using the golden mean [a ratio of approximately 0.616 to 1.000] to derive proportion."

The Main Street Collection.
Designed by John Hutton, 1978-1979.
Manufactured by Donghia Furniture.
Materials: horsehair or foam (no CFCs), muslin and wool batting or dacron, unbleached cotton batting, hand-tied coil springs, feather and down, kiln-dried hardwood frame with double-doweled construction. Collection includes: Main Street Sofa, Main Street Club Sofa, Main Street Club Chair and Ottoman.

Designed when Donghia was commissioned to re-outfit the S.S. France to become the S.S. Norway, the largest cruise ship ever built.

Photography by Scott Frances

The Enchanted Collection.
Designed by John Hutton, 1990-1991.
Manufactured by Donghia Furniture.
Materials: horsehair or foam (no CFCs),
muslin and wool batting or dacron,
unbleached cotton batting, hand-tied coil
springs, feather and down, kiln-dried
hardwood frame with double-doweled
construction. Collection includes: Spirit
Sofa, the Ghost Chair, the Phantom
Chairs, the Casper Chairs, and the
Illusion Bench.

   "The inspiration for this design
occurred on the open porch of my country
house on Long Island. In the fall I cover
the ornate Victorian wicker furniture on
the porch with sheets. One fall evening as
I was doing so there was a slight breeze as
I covered my wife Brenda's English Racer
with a sheet. Because of the configuration
of the handle bars draped in the sheets
and the movement from the breeze it
looked to me like an angel. I turned to
see the other shapes on the porch and
found all of these huge pieces stripped of
their detail by the drape of the sheets.
From this enchanting scene the collection
was born."

—John Hutton

Photography by Elizabeth Heyert

The Haute Chair. Designed by John
Hutton, 1992. Manufactured by
Donghia Furniture. Materials: horsehair
or foam (no CFCs), muslin and wool
batting or dacron, unbleached cotton batting, hand-tied coil springs, feather and
down, kiln-dried hardwood frame with
double-doweled construction.

   Designed for a former employee at
Donghia, Sheilah Puckett, a petite
woman with the type of stature often
overlooked in furniture design. These
pieces are comfortable for tall people as
well, but the reverse is rarely true. Very
feminine, provocative, and reflective of a
woman of great style. A short skirt and
open pleats at the corners reveal an
undergarment.
Photography by Scott Frances

Michael Wolk

PHOTOGRAPHY BY DONNA VICTOR

Michael Wolk of Miami draws from many sources for his furniture designs—the classics from Bauhaus to Shaker to Art Deco—and combines them in unlikely (but likable) partnerships. Whatever the root for a particular piece, it is bound to be irreverent yet elegant.

Michael Wolk Design Associates opened in 1984 following ten years during which Wolk worked with various companies practicing interior and industrial design as well as the design of graphics. A graduate of Pratt Institute where he received a Bachelor of Industrial Design degree with honors in 1973, Wolk has received many awards for his work including the 1992 first place award in the CODA/HD Furniture Competition and three first place awards for his furniture designs in the 1992 Florida Style Furniture Design Competition.

"My degree is in industrial design. Materials and methods of manufacturing were an integral part of that training. Much of my work is now in the field of interior design. The parameter of a particular client's needs always impacts the end result. The client needing the furniture to function becomes the guiding principle."

"Most important to me is that the furniture I design feed the left and right side of my brain."

"The responsibility of the designer is to meet the functional, structural and aesthetic requirements of each particular design as it relates to the client, users or society."

The Weber Chair. Designed by Michael Wolk, 1993. Manufactured by Preview Furniture Corp. Customer's own material. Exposed legs and arms: shown in maple; available in custom finishes. First place award: 1993 Florida Style Furniture Design Competition. Photography by Donna Victor

The Miami Chair. Designed by Michael Wolk. Manufactured by Preview Furniture Corp., 1993. Fully upholstered seat and back. Customer's own material. Grand Prize: 1990 Florida Style Furniture Design Competition. Photography by Bob Gelberg

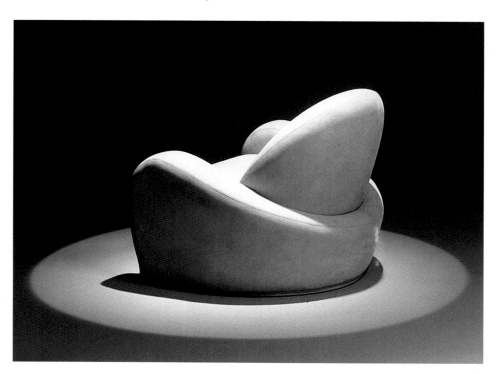

Miro Highback. Designed by Michael Wolk, 1993. Manufactured by Stansson Studio. Fully upholstered seat and back, customer's own material. Exposed legs: shown in oak; available in custom finishes. Photography by Seth Benson

Afra and Tobia Scarpa

Afra Bianchin was born in Montebelluna, Tobia Scarpa in Venice. They started working professionally in Venice in 1958, gaining experience with glass at the Venini glassworks. In 1959 they designed for Franco Albini's course at the Venice Faculty of Architecture, where they were students, their first chair to be put into production, first by the firm Santabona, then by Gavina. The fruitful working relationship that began with the latter firm in 1960 led to successes such as the sofa Bastiano and the bed Vanessa. In the same year Flos asked them to design some lamps, which marked the beginning of constant relations resulting in lamps such as Fantasma, Jucker, Ariette and Papillona right up to the latest ones, Butterfly and Pierrot. Work began for Cassina just a few years later, in 1963, and gave them the opportunity of designing a complex and refined collection of residential furniture, including the armchair 925, now in the permanent collection of the Museum of Modern Art in New York.

During the '80s all their experiences were subjected to deep self-reflection, which transformed their immense mastery of the components involved in a

project into a quality that could have lasting value, ignoring the ultra-consumeristic trend of the time.

Highlights of their prolific production during those years and now have been: furniture for Casas and Meritalia; office furniture for Unifor, B&B Italia Office Division and IB Office; many restoration projects; new construction in Italy and abroad; exhibit and shop design for B&B Italia, Unifor and Benetton with whom they have had a decades' long relationship; vases for Veart; silverware for San Lorenzo; fireplace accessories for Dimensione Fuoco; and colored steel shingles for Veas.

"Designing, or rather knowing how to design, is the most complex and complete answer to man's wish to be able to see the effect his actions have in the future. This is the reason man has developed suitable capacities and instruments.

"Making furniture for the architect (for us there is no substantial difference between interior designing and structural projects) does not just mean thinking about the objects, but simultaneously thinking about the technical requests that the manufacturer will be making to be able to reach a vital equilibrium between the chosen materials, the production techniques and the necessary investment costs."

"We have always put ourselves to the test when designing, to bring about interactions between function, use, working technique and form, as a final striking element, in such a way that the concept of style, personal form and other things do not have any sense, although they are there all the same because of necessity."

"The designer's responsibility is non-physical longevity. In other words...the Socratic good and beauty."

Ronda. *Designed by Afra and Tobia Scarpa, 1986. Manufactured by Casas. Armchair and two or three seated divan. Steel structure. The filler and the cushions are in polyurethane and Dacron. Base in anthracite aluminum and feet in poliamide. Covering is in leather or fabric. Photography by Sergio Efrem Raimondi*

Gitana. Designed by Afra and Tobia
Scarpa, 1993. Manufactured by
Meritalia. Armchair built with four
tubular steel frames. Seat backs, seats and
armrests are independent and kept with a
system of elastic belting and with elastic
joints at the bases. They are filled with
variable density synthetic batting, so the
single components can respond to movement with elasticity.
Photography by Marco Schillaci

Veneziana. Designed by Afra and
Tobia Scarpa, 1991. Manufactured by
Casas. Armchair and two or three seated
divan. Structure in steel. Dacron and
polyurethane foam batting. Base in
anthracite aluminum. Feet in poliamide.
Photography by Sergio Efrem Raimondi

Sandra Nunnerly

*S*andra Nunnerly is as fascinated by luxurious icons of the past as she is with the well-edited simplicity she considers in keeping with today's lifestyles, and she sees no reason why one can't have both. Neither do her clients. In fact, the grand overtones of the furniture, fabrics and accessories she designed for Escada's private salon in Manhattan were met with such a positive response that she has developed them into a line for the retail market. With an almost Yin and Yang opposition of design elements, she blends the past and the present by playing her fabrics of freshly contemporary stripes and florals against an array of traditionally designed sofas and chairs that would have enticed Louis XVI to come shopping.

In her own home in New York, the materials are still rich and her custom upholstered pieces embellished with luxurious trimmings, but the color

palette is pared down to one tone—ivory. It exudes feelings of airy comfort, welcome and warmth, yet every vignette is picture-perfect as well.

After obtaining her Bachelor of Fine Arts degree in Architecture from the University of Sydney, Australia, Nunnerly moved to New York City and worked with the Marlborough and Nancy Hoffman Galleries before establishing her own design firm in 1981. Sandra Nunnerly Inc. handles a wide range of residential and corporate commissions, and Nunnerly also has been active in product development in both the design of furniture and fabric lines.

"I suppose my having been at one time an art gallery director affects my work including my furniture design as much as my background in architecture and interiors. However, the function of furniture, how it works with the body, has to be as pleasing as its visual effect."

"Strange as it may seem, because it can be extremely tortuous trying to communicate your ideas to someone else, the fabrication is perhaps my favorite part of furniture design. Working with my craftsmen brings me great joy, as does seeing my design on paper come to life as a real object. So many things on paper never do!"

"One of the major responsibilities of the designer is to answer the needs of the time. I design spaces and furniture for people living in the 1990s. Very few of them have formal dining rooms, yet many enjoy the feeling of grandeur. Very few have much space, so what they do have has to be flexible. I particularly like designing a small space and filling it with all the right things...furniture which is satisfying, both emotionally and functionally."

High-Backed Striped Chair and fabrics, *1992. Created by Sandra Nunnerly for Escada's private salon in Manhattan in 1992, now available through the designer on a custom basis. Photography © by David Letendre*

Milo Baughman

*M*ilo Baughman began his distinguished career in California in 1947 as both an interior and furniture designer. Quickly becoming identified with the burgeoning California Modern trend, he launched many lines for various national manufacturers, becoming most closely identified with Thayer Coggin, Inc., with whom he has been associated since 1953. Other clients are Tropitone, Garden Source, the Naturalist, and Lister, a U.K. company. Known also as an educator, he currently serves as adjunct professor in the Department of Design, Brigham Young University, Provo, Utah.

In 1987 Baughman was honored by the American Society of Furniture Designers with the Distinguished Designer Award, which initiates him into the Furniture Designer's Hall of Fame.

Light Wave Collection. *Designed by Milo Baughman, 1992. Manufactured by Thayer Coggin. The series includes twelve pieces, including a chaise, sofas, chairs and a group of tables. Legs available in Thayer Coggin lacquer colors or wood finishes.*
Photography by Mark Peterson/Albion Associates

"Staying involved with interior design whenever time allows has helped me to develop a sense of what really works, and what really pleases the occupants of a house. If I didn't know or care how my furniture is used—how it solves problems and how it meets genuine human needs—I would become concerned only with Design-for-Design's-Sake; I would concentrate on turning out 'museum pieces' and end up not giving a fig whether my furniture served real purposes for real people, but only if it won recognition. This can be a fatal temptation for many designers. I know. I've struggled with it myself."

"It's difficult to separate design from fabrication from function. Design, if it's to be successful, must be functional, but defining 'function' in the present postmodern era no longer needs to be as dogmatically and narrowly defined as it once was. A Mexican designer friend of mine once told me, 'Even perfume is functional.' What he meant is that beyond pure utility, to evoke the right emotional response sometimes serves a greater purpose than to merely make sure that the object 'works.'

"Fabrication is of course very important. Furniture that appears initially to work, as well as to evoke the desired (and we always hope valid) emotional response, but falls apart shortly after purchase, is an unmitigated scam."

"The responsible designer must be very aware of ergonomic issues, which presently go far beyond the study of kinetics and merely providing good lumbar support in task chairs. The terms 'Humanistic Design' and 'Green Design' are now part of the overall ergonomic concern. Psychological comfort and safety are equally important considerations. In its more common use, 'Green Design' is more explicitly concerned with questions of stewardship—the prudent selection and use of materials: Is the wood used an endangered species? Are the plastic components recyclable? Are the fabrics made of essentially natural fibers?"

Noel Jeffrey

*oel Jeffrey admires classical architecture and the late eighteenth century (primarily French). Yet the "less is more" philosophy of Le Corbusier has a place in his heart, too. And the furniture as well as interiors designed by Noel Jeffrey reflect them all. The main thing, says this New Yorker, is that each piece be appropriate for the space…and beautiful!

Jeffrey is known for his fluency in a broad range of styles and his distinctive ability to create environments that are both inviting and adventuresome. His commissions have included domestic and commercial interiors as well as model apartments for prominent developers. Unusual juxtapositions and historical references are two of his trademarks, as well as the many custom pieces he designs for his clients. These are usually neoclassical in style, such as tables with inlaid woods and gilding along with rolled armed and Regency sofas.

He studied at Pratt Institute, and took additional architectural studies at Columbia University before opening Noel Jeffrey, Inc. in 1969.

"When I design furniture, I use my knowledge of interior design to form the parameters of each piece. If it is a chair, then I need to decide what level of comfort is to be established. That can range from a very comfortable club chair to a highly designed chair for a hall that is more sculpture than chair. If I'm designing a table, then I must decide how the piece fits into a room. Is the table small, such as an end table?…or large, such as a center hall or dining table? After deciding on the size, I determine the design of the table and its suitability to the overall appearance of the room."

"I really feel that all three aspects of furniture design— design, function and fabrication—are very important. Just as all the function will determine the design, the fabrication will assure that the design satisfies the function. No matter how well designed a piece of furniture is, it is the execution of the design that will insure its success."

"The responsibility of the designer is to create furniture that is both pleasing to the eye and fulfills its function without flaw."

Egyptian Revival Style Tufted Chaise.
Rope and tassel detailing and gold leaf sabots. Upholstered in white cotton matelassé. Designed by Noel Jeffrey, 1988. Special order through Noel Jeffrey, Inc. Photography by Peter Vitale/courtesy of Noel Jeffrey, Inc.

Three Seat Sofa. *Abbreviated rolled arms, gold leaf feet, and upholstered in taupe mohair. Designed by Noel Jeffrey, 1989. Special order through Noel Jeffrey, Inc. Photography by Alex McLean/Courtesy of Noel Jeffrey, Inc.*

Regency Style Two Seat Sofa. Decorative arm rolls, tassels and gilt acorn feet. Designed by Noel Jeffrey, 1989. Special order through Noel Jeffrey, Inc. Photography courtesy of Noel Jeffrey, Inc.

Art Deco Style Lounge Chair. Curved mahogany platform base, upholstered in peacock blue velvet. Designed by Noel Jeffrey, 1984. Special order through Noel Jeffrey, Inc. Photography courtesy of Noel Jeffrey, Inc.

Adam Tihany

*A*dam Tihany, designer of commercial and residential interiors, has been articulating his designs in Europe and the United States for the past fifteen years. Tihany is a graduate of the Italian Politecnico di Milano, School of Architecture and Urban Planning.

Both nationally and internationally acclaimed, Tihany is considered one of the foremost hospitality designers in America today. He is credited with many award-winning restaurants. With partner and chef Francesco Antonucci, he opened the Remi New York to considerable accolades for its unique design and Venetian cuisine. Others include Bicé worldwide, Remi (New York, Santa Monica, Mexico City and Tel Aviv), Spago Las Vegas, Le Cirque, Biba and Huberts.

His hotel projects include: the five-hundred-room Doubletree, California; the presidential suites at Bally's Park Place Casino Hotel, Atlantic City; the

lobby and lounge of the Drake Suissotel, New York City; Dan Hotels, Israel; and a golf and conference center, Golf de Fregate, France.

Tihany also designs furniture and accessory lines. Among the most recognized are the Trocadero Collection manufactured in the U.S. under licensing by Shelby Williams, the Il Mago series and the

Archipiatti plate series for Villeroy and Boch, and the Grande Lounge Collection and the Venezia line for Pace.

The Grand Lounge Collection was inspired by the Grand Lounge of the S.S. *Normandie*, a luxury cruise ship of the 1930s. The collection represents Tihany's first collaboration with an American furniture company, and it was unveiled in 1990 at the Pace New York showroom.

> *"Having an in-depth understanding of space and scale is an essential ingredient to the successful design of furniture."*

> *"The three categories—design, fabrication and function—are equally important and sometimes inseparable. The ultimate challenge is to combine successfully functional challenges with innovative manufacturing methods and new design solutions."*

> *"Through the use of 'objects and things' the designer has the opportunity to influence people's lives…at home, at the workplace, at leisure…. The philosophical responsibility is certainly to make the world a better place in which to live."*

Gertrude, a lounge chair. Designed by Adam Tihany, 1990. Manufactured by The Pace Collection. Curved arms of black matte with a burl frame. Seat and back cushions available in fabric or leather upholstery. The ottoman is composed of four legs in a black matte finish. The upholstered cushion is framed in burl. Photography courtesy of The Pace Collection

Rebecca. Designed by Adam Tihany, 1990. Manufactured by The Pace Collection. Gently curved slat back. Available in mahogany, black matte or cherry finish, with optional contrasting finish on the slats. Seat cushion is upholstered in fabric or leather. Photography courtesy of The Pace Collection

Marnie, a club chair. *Designed by Adam Tihany, 1990. Manufactured by The Pace Collection. Curved frame with tapered saddle leather posts. Upholstered in fabric or leather with a loose seat cushion. Photography courtesy of The Pace Collection*

Collete. *Designed by Adam Tihany, 1990. Manufactured by The Pace Collection. Composed of three tapered legs with a round upholstered seat framed in elm burl. The curved seat back is also detailed in elm burl. Upholstery available in fabric or leather. Photography courtesy of The Pace Collection*

Toshiyuki Kita

*A*ctive internationally as an environmental and product designer, Osaka and Milan-based architect Toshiyuki Kita is also involved with traditional Japanese craft design such as lacquer ware and traditional Japanese paper products.

Two of his works have been selected as part of the permanent collection of the Museum of Modern Art in New York. In 1983 he received a product design award from the Institute of Business Designers and *Contract* magazine in the United States. In 1984 he was awarded first prize in the Residential Furnishing category by *Industrial Design* magazine. In 1987 he took part in the celebrations of the Centre Georges Pompidou's tenth anniversary in Paris, and in 1990 he was awarded the Delta de Oro in Spain.

Kita completed a degree in Industrial Design at Naniwa College in Osaka in 1964. He established his design office in 1967 and began working in Italy as well as Japan in 1969.

"My work varies from product design to space design. I believe that every design should relate to people's life-style. Particularly, furniture design should be an extension of the human body."

"The vital element of design should be the balance of its function and its looks and its cost. It is important to design an object that can be used comfortably by many people."

"The earth is reaching close to a critical stage. As my occupation is to design products for mass production, I feel a responsibility in designing products that are ecologically friendly."

Fido. *Designed by Toshiyuki Kita, 1990. Body: Polyurethane foam upholstered with fabric. Front leg: Wood. Back leg: Aluminum cast. Manufactured by Moroso s.p.s. Photography courtesy of Moroso*

Times. *Designed by Toshiyuki Kita, 1991. Body: Polyurethane foam upholstered with fabric or leather. Manufactured by Cassina s.p.a. Photography courtesy of Cassina*

Ronn Jaffe

PHOTOGRAPHY BY MARK WIELAND

Ronn Jaffe is an interior designer, artist, businessman and lecturer, and is gaining recognition as a prolific furniture designer as well. Formally trained in fine arts from age ten to fifteen at the Corcoran School of Art in Washington, D.C., Jaffe proceeded to earn a degree in marketing from Boston University. He went on to study at the Harvard Graduate School of Design and the Boston Museum School.

Jaffe says his design philosophy evolved from this juxtaposition of business and artistic idioms and has directed his approach as president of the interior design firm Ronn Jaffe Incorporated, founded in 1970 with his partner/wife Mars Jaffe. Clients have included Fortune 500 companies such as Shell Oil, the Kellogg Corporation, Thiokol, U.S. West, and the Rouse Company.

In most of his interiors, whether office or residential design, there is an emphasis on custom-designed and handcrafted furnishings. "Interior design is all about making people feel as good as they possibly can in their surroundings, and meeting their individual needs," he says.

"Being an interior designer enhances my perspective as a furniture designer. There is a considerable benefit in having a pragmatic and artistic understanding and everyday working knowledge of furniture's relationship to the interior environment. The key is integration. Furniture is only one part of the mix of many elements that comprise a complete interior. Being a purchaser and specifier of furniture provides a firsthand awareness of market needs, desires and trends."

"All three elements in this triumvirate—design, function and fabrication—must be in harmonious balance.

"But if I had to say which to me is most important—design and detail always."

"The designer's responsibility? Integrity and commitment to the design, the product and the user as well as a sensitivity to prevalent social values."

Messa Slipper Chair. Designed by Ronn Jaffe, 1989. Horsehair fabric with leather welt trim and leather tassels. Shown with Y-Fret Table of wood with ebony and white lacquer finish and copper leaf circle inset. Designed by Jaffe in 1988. Available in several combinations of lacquer paint colors and gold, silver or copper metal leaf through Ronn Jaffe Incorporated.
Photography by Mark Wieland

Blush Lounge Chair, with Blush Foot Stool/Ottoman. Designed by Ronn Jaffe, 1990. Rose-hued mohair plush with mahogany wood legs. Shown with Ra Pedestal of polychrome wood, travertine marble top, gold leaf feet. Designed by Jaffe in 1984. Available in custom colors and wood finishes with a variety of stone and wood tops through Ronn Jaffe Incorporated.
Photography by Mark Wieland

Shepard Vineburg

*T*here is a dynamic, sculptural look to everything that comes out of this Los Angeles designer's architectural and interior design studio. His approach stems from his perspective that the classics which stand the test of time are born of three ingredients—purity and simplicity of line, durability of construction, and the ability to adapt into many settings.

Vineburg studied at Pratt Institute and the New York School of Interior Design and has lectured at the Fashion Institute of Design and Merchandising and the Rudolph Schaeffer School of Design, both in San Francisco. Previous to establishing his own firm in 1991, he was affiliated with Skidmore, Owings and Merrill, San Francisco; Whisler-Patri, San Francisco; and Erika Brunson Design Associates, Los Angeles.

"Good design encompasses all aspects of the design process. As well-engineered design is based on 'form follows function,' exemplary fabrication is based on how well the designer has analyzed how the object will be used and the amount of wear and tear it will undergo. One hopes to design a product that will age well, with a patina, rather than becoming tomorrow's white elephant."

Myra Armchair. *Designed by Shepard Vineburg, 1991. For desk or dining. Available through Randolph & Hein and Holly Hunt showrooms. Photography by Philip Thompson*

Simone Sofa. *Designed by Shepard Vineburg, 1991. Available through Randolph & Hein and Holly Hunt showrooms. "Discus" legs are 22k giltwood. Shown with large Discus Table Lamp and Clipper Lamp Table. Photography by Philip Thompson*

Coldwater Canyon Residence, *Los Angeles, California. Designed by Shepard Vineburg, 1993, including his custom upholstery, Olympic Floor Lamp with tray table, and small Discus Table Lamp of giltwood. All available through Randolph & Hein and Holly Hunt showrooms. Photography by Andy Knudson-Davey*

Michael Graves

Michael Graves has been in the forefront of architectural design since the beginning of his practice in 1964. His work has directly influenced the transformation of urban architecture from the abstract "Modern Architecture" toward more contextual and traditional themes. In his projects, Graves has consistently demonstrated his ability to create designs sympathetic to both the general program of use and the context of the site.

As president and principal architect of Michael Graves, Architect, P.A., in Princeton, New Jersey, Graves has produced designs for more than two hundred projects including interior spaces of most of his buildings.

After receiving a Bachelor of Science in Architecture from the University of Cincinnati in 1958, Graves continued his education at Harvard University where he received a Master of Architecture in 1959 and at the American Academy in Rome where he was a Fellow from 1960 to 1962.

"As an architect, I find myself interested in the artifacts of daily life and how they can be related to architecture. Because I see architecture and design as part of the same aesthetic continuum, I think it's unnecessary to distinguish between making a space, a build-

ing or a piece of furniture, aside from their more obvious differences of program and scale. What is important in all of this work is that there is a consciousness or sense of the domestic, a consciousness that informs and enriches design at all scales."

"Good design is an all-encompassing idea; it has many components and they all must work in unison. For this reason, it doesn't seem right to give precedence to one aspect of a design over another, because inevitably you will be sacrificing something. The challenge of design is addressing and working out all of its many concerns, from function to appearance to fabrication. The way in which a product is manufactured, how it works and what it looks like are fundamentally tied together. You can't separate them from one another."

"Design is, in part, both a reflection and a recognition of one's own time and history. You cannot ignore the concerns of the day. At present in particular, issues such as political correctness and ecology have become important to many designers, just as they have similarly come to affect other areas of public and private life. However, I don't think you can allow these concerns to become metaphors for design. In such cases, the issue of the moment frequently becomes no more than a device for marketing the product as opposed to an element or aspect of its overall design. I think that issues like these are best suited to informing design and improving it. They shouldn't become the raison d'être of a work."

Graves Lounge Chair. *Designed by Michael Graves, 1989. Manufactured by Spinneybeck Design America. Leather square feet. Spinneybeck leather or customer's own material. Ottoman also available.*
Photography by Marek Bulaj

Charles A. Reimann

*F*rom early childhood when he was playing with Lego and imagining dominoes were black leather sofas with white buttons, Charles A. Reimann has been fascinated by every aspect of interior design.

"Looking at the shapes and forms of the freeway overpasses from the back window of my dad's car, I knew I would be in a career that involved art and design," he says.

Growing up in Michigan, then moving to England to live with his aunt, he met a furniture maker, later to become his father-in-law, who taught Reimann everything he could about furniture design and manufacturing. Later, when Reimann returned to Hawaii where his father was born and raised, he met Brian Mikami, a highly skilled upholsterer with whom he formed a partnership and opened his first design studio. When they added partner Norman Rosa, they decided to go national with their designs and products. Reimann Mikami now has a manufacturing facility in Seattle and representatives in a select few other U.S. cities.

"I am an interior designer and that's what gives me my drive and imagination in furniture design. I feel all my clients should be presented with much more than hospitality catalog furniture. Soon I'll be able to offer them the textiles I'm designing for my furniture as well."

"The designer's responsibility? To provide the client with furniture that's constructed well, proportioned in scale with the interior, has the proper comfort and is designed in a style that can be appreciated and stand on its own merit."

Spike, Pike and Cenci *(from left). Designed by Charles A. Reimann in 1988, 1990, and 1991 respectively. Manufactured by Reimann Mikami, Inc. Leather. With polished stainless steel discs (Pike and Spike) and brushed aluminum frame (Cenci). Photography by Christopher Barrett/Kingfish Photography*

Robert Stuffings

*R*obert Stuffings, who resides in Sarasota, Florida, where he has designed and is presently building his fourth Palladian-inspired residence, has been involved in residential architecture and interior design for twenty years and has completed projects on a national level.

Through much of his work there is a constant element which links his architecture, interiors and furniture to the past. "It is my belief that, in a world so 'charged' by cataclysmic events unfolding unceasingly through electronic media and where values have become transitory, my work should reflect a historic 'anchor,' " he says. "It is my intention that my architecture, interiors and furnishings retain a feeling of peace and permanence and imbue the human spirit with respect."

"My training and experience have allowed me to study and understand structure. Through this knowledge one becomes adept at understanding the mathematical relationships that underlie structure and its relevance to supportive and nurturing designs for human beings."

"Paramount consideration is always given to function. Once all the criteria as to how the piece is to be used are identified, fabrication can then be altered to support the requirements of the finished article. The initial design or concept is always refined to meet the needs of an article's function and fabrication."

" 'Integrity' is the responsibility of any designer, especially as it pertains to creating products that fulfill a specific need. By maintaining 'integrity' in design, the creator is naturally sensitive to employing ecologically sound materials and specifying a degree of craftsmanship that allows the article to endure."

The Robert Stuffings Collection.
Designed by Robert Stuffings, 1990. Manufactured by A. Rudin. Down and 100 percent silk. Collection includes sofas and upholstered chairs. Shown in Stuffings' Palladian-inspired residence which he designed and built in Osprey (near Sarasota), Florida. Photography by Dan Forer

Lauren Rottet

*L*auren Rottet is Interiors Partner of Keating Mann Jernigan Rottet, a Los Angeles-based architectural and interiors firm with national and international projects. A registered architect, Rottet's experience encompasses major architectural, planning and interiors projects.

After graduating with honors from the University of Texas, Rottet joined Fisher Friedman & Associates, San Francisco. A ten-year period in the Chicago, Houston and Los Angeles offices of Skidmore, Owings & Merrill followed. Prior to forming Keating Mann Jernigan Rottet, Lauren Rottet joined the firm's other partners in assuming leadership of SOM's Los Angeles office where she was Associate Partner and Head of Interior Design.

"As an architect and interior designer who specifies large amounts of furniture, I am aware of what is missing in the marketplace, not only from a functional standpoint but also from a visual standpoint. Furniture design for me came naturally from searching for specific products for specific locations and not finding the right piece—as a result we design it, whether it is a reception desk, secretarial desk, case goods or lounge furniture. My belief is that architecture and design do not stop at the walls—they go to the details of furnishings and accessories."

"The design of furniture is a combination of the function, visual aspect and the ease of fabrication. Especially in today's marketplace, furniture must be competitively priced. To achieve this, the product must be easy to fabricate, with the ability to reduce numbers of custom pieces. For this reason, I believe in working with the manufacturer to achieve a design that is easy to fabricate, well engineered, and durable. The function is the impetus for the design, but the engineering of the fabrication process must follow."

"In my opinion, the designer has the responsibility to produce a product that will be long lasting, both in design and in quality. A well-designed product can be used for years, looking fresh and functioning well. I still specify some pieces which were designed in the twenties and they are still fresh and beautiful. Well-designed furniture can be moved from office to office or home to home, adapting well. Poorly designed furniture becomes dated and is often thrown out, which is not ecologically or economically desirable. Furniture must also be flexible so it can be used in different situations. This was the basis for Evaneau with parts and pieces which can be reupholstered separately for a fresh image. The pieces are varied, asymmetrical, symmetrical, sofas, corner chairs, lounge chairs and ottomans...all combining to make flexible groupings."

***Evaneau Lounge Seating**. Designed by Lauren Rottet, 1992. Manufactured by Brayton International, Inc. Leather: Brayton. Fabric: Design Tex. Shown with Biarritz Table by Brayton against a projected image of the Pierre Koenig Case Study House #22 and a vintage Hollywood Storefront backdrop at the Brayton temporary showroom space, also designed by Rottet, at WestWeek '93, Los Angeles.*
Photography by Roland Bishop

Evaneau Seating. Designed by Lauren Rottet, 1992. Manufactured by Brayton International, Inc. Fabrics: Design Tex. Shown in the Brayton temporary showroom space, also designed by Rottet, at WestWeek '92.
Photography by Roland Bishop

Evaneau Lounge Seating. Designed by Lauren Rottet, 1992. Manufactured by Brayton International, Inc. Fabrics: Knoll (blue velvet), Clarence House (checkerboard fabric), Brayton (blue leather). Shown with Wellaver tables by Brayton against a projected image of a house designed by architect Richard Neutra and a vintage Hollywood backdrop at the Brayton temporary showroom space, also designed by Rottet, at WestWeek '93, Los Angeles.
Photography by Roland Bishop

Larry Totah

Totah Design is diversified, unconventional and eclectic. Whether creating furniture design or the entire interior space, its founder Larry Totah is recognized for not subscribing to set standards. No wonder his international recognition is equaled by his popularity nearer his home-base in Los Angeles—with Totah Design Furniture now a valuable rental source for motion pictures, commercials and photography studios.

Totah studied architecture and design at the University of Houston, the University of California, Los Angeles, and the Southern California Institute of Architecture. He opened Totah Design in 1981 and its services include commercial and residential design as well as furniture design. Notable public projects by the firm include Maxfield/Yohji Yamamoto and People Clothing Store in West Hollywood, California, Noa Noa Restaurant in Beverly Hills, and Odeum in Japan.

"Being an interior designer as well as product designer gives me a tighter control of the entire space. It enables me to create a more unique, individualized aesthetic."

"I believe all aspects of furniture design—the design, the function and the fabrication—are equally important. It's really relative to each individual situation and how I approach it. It could be through the design or fabrication whereby a discovery is made in the process, or through the function whereby individuals are moved by the way a piece works."

"The need for which something is created determines everything else. Sometimes the need doesn't allow for ergonomics or longevity or even ecology to become paramount. It is up to the designer to take these into account and do the best he or she can."

Round Chair. *Designed by Larry Totah, 1992. From the Neo Geo collection. Represented by Diva, Los Angeles; Archetype Gallery, New York; and Limn, San Francisco.*
Photography by Douglas Hill

Wave Sectional. *Designed by Larry Totah, 1985. Fabricated as a single unit, as two separate pieces (shown), or as part of a three-piece wave with a center module. Represented by Diva, Los Angeles; Archetype Gallery, New York; and Limn, San Francisco.*
Photography by Analisa Pessin

T.P. Chair. *Designed by Larry Totah, 1986. Represented by Diva, Los Angeles; Archetype Gallery, New York; and Limn, San Francisco.*
Photography by Analisa Pessin

Vidy Split. *Designed by Larry Totah, 1992. From the Neo Geo collection. Represented by Diva, Los Angeles; Archetype Gallery, New York; and Limn, San Francisco.*
Photography by Douglas Hill

Harry Segil

*O*ne has to stretch one's imagination to understand how a Harry Segil design might fit into a somewhat normal life—and that is just what Segil (a.k.a. HaRry) has been asking his clients to do before they even think of purchasing one of his colorfully energetic furniture events—to be imaginative.

A native of South Africa, Segil's aesthetic celebrates Africa's bold sense of color, texture and style—a style that has many parallels with California's

piece of pop culture and the American dream. In 1980, Segil moved to Los Angeles to practice interior design and, trading on his expertise in antiques from the seventeenth to the twentieth century, to open the HaRry Antique Warehouse. Yet almost immediately he began creating his own pieces, distinctly contemporary odes to a variety of styles from the past.

Today HaRry offers a complete product line as well as custom pieces for commercial and residential settings. Every piece is made by hand.

"Being an interior designer gives me the crucial understanding of the importance of creating furniture that works in a living or working environment and solves problems that people have (such as space, specific uses, new technology). It allows me to understand how people live and relate to their environments, plus a lot of practical information on what people actually need in their environments and what is not available and needs to be designed to fulfill their needs. It also gives me the understanding of how important it is to create furniture that is not only practical but also can offer much more—energy, fun, art inspiration, new ideas, emotional support. Life in the '90s is hard and brutal and your environment is your castle and it should be a safe, cozy place of refuge."

"For me function is of primary importance. Unless the furniture is made to be comfortable for the use for which it is intended, it serves no purpose. People do not have space for furniture objects that are merely conversation pieces. Naturally each piece should be well constructed and durable. However, design is also the magical element to stimulate and inspire people into thinking and reassessing the way we see things and opening their eyes to new ideas and new uses of materials."

"It is absolutely essential to design furniture that is consumer friendly and respects the comfort and support of the human body."

Cloud Chaise. *Designed by Harry Segil, 1992. Shown in multi-colored Naugahyde; also available in customer's own material.*
Photography by Harry Segil

Queen Mary Channel Back Love Seat. *Designed by Harry Segil, 1987. Shown in multi-colored Naugahyde; also available in customer's own fabric.*
Photography by Harry Segil

Fan Chair and Vanite Chair.

Designed by Harry Segil, 1988 and 1993 respectively. Fan Chair: upholstered in colored Naugahyde with lacquered wood detail. Available through HaRry Showroom. Vanite Chair: One of a kind; upholstered in vinyl and antique textiles; lacquered wood legs. Lacquered free-form table on metal legs, designed by Harry Segil, 1993.
Photography by Jeff Eichen

Galactica Chair. *Designed by Harry Segil, 1992. Shown with wool upholstery; also available in customer's own fabric. Chrome plated metal legs.*
Photography by Jeff Eichen

Queen Mary Pop Brite Chair.

Designed by Harry Segil, 1991. Shown in multi-colored Naugahyde; also available in customer's own fabric.
Photography by Jeff Eichen

Ergo Design Works
Lory Johansson · June Robinson

A romantic eccentricity marks the interiors and furniture designed by Ergo's Lory Johansson and June Robinson, who are finding an appreciative audience among their celebrity clientele in Los Angeles. A duck-footed ottoman and double-sided sofa are just two examples of the way they mix whimsical sentiment with a strong sense of passionate adventure.

Ergo Design Works, Inc. was founded in 1991 after Johansson *(left)* and

Robinson *(right)*, from California and Scotland respectively, had worked as a successful design team for two years. Their service covers all aspects of the design spectrum, from concept, through working and presentation drawings, to project implementation and final completion.

"Being interior designers allows us to work on an intimate level with a cross section of clientele, opening a window and shedding light on personal needs. As designers of entire rooms, we have an opportunity to create furniture that is intensely personal...that reflects the harmony and scale of the rooms themselves...which conveys the personality and inner nuances (be they playful or serious) of the people for whom it is being designed."

"Design, fabrication and function are all interdependent factors. The most exciting of these is, of course, the design. When we know the use intended for a piece, we can abstract the idea by, at times, pulling thoughts from the ether (sometimes literally in dreams) or from our vast mind library of things known and some half-forgotten. All of this plus a little bit of fun combines to form the design. Once we get it down on paper we hand it over to only the best workmen with strict instructions so that the result we imagined can be realized."

"Designers' responsibility is to their clients, whether commercial or residential. Clients' needs are paramount...any piece of furniture designed for them must be made to the highest possible standards. No matter how ornate, our furniture, unless requested to be otherwise, is always made to be part of the environment, and to us the greatest compliment is to hear that friends and family of our clients use and enjoy our work."

Duck-Footed Ottoman. *Designed by Lory Johansson and June Robinson/Ergo Design Works, 1993. Gilt foot, customer's own fabric. Distributed by Frewil Inc.*
Photography by Kenneth Johansson

PHOTOGRAPHY BY MARK HARMEL

Double-Sided Sofa. Designed by Lory
Johansson and June Robinson/Ergo
Design Works, 1992. Mahogany frame,
customer's own fabric. Available through
the designers.
Photography by Kenneth Johansson

Peter Shelton and Lee F. Mindel

*T*hese two New Yorkers have never stopped studying, learning and exploring since they established their firm in 1978. "The only thing that's constant in architecture is change," says Mindel.

Shelton studied architecture at the University of Pennsylvania and Pratt Institute where he received his degree in 1975. He worked for the New York architectural firms of Edward Durell Stone & Associates and Emery

Roth & Sons prior to his founding the present organization.

Mindel received his Masters of Architecture from Harvard University in 1976 after obtaining his Bachelor of Arts cum laude with Distinction in Architecture at the University of Pennsylvania. He worked for the New York architecture firms of Skidmore, Owings & Merrill and Rogers, Butler, Burgun.

"To provide architectural, interior and product design for corporate, retail and residential clients, you have to keep examining where you are and if you're truly solving problems appropriately. If you solve a problem appropriately, you've created something of value, something that lasts forever.

"For us the only way to arrive at such appropriateness is to start with the architecture. Everything comes from architecture and an understanding of all that means. Furniture and all the ideas generated to fill space have to do with the space itself. Therefore, it's not happenstance that all of our furniture design has come from designing real environments for real clients. To us it couldn't be any other way, because we know that it's so necessary to consider the total space. Good furniture design can't be arbitrary. It can't come from designing in a vacuum. Each piece within a space is a brush stroke of a larger canvas."

"The key is integration of all the disciplines. This includes site planning and plantscape as well as the architecture and interior. If there's a dialogue and the conscious integration of all the elements, you can then create a seamless environment, and also an environment which is greater than the sum of its parts."

"Appropriate design is that which relates to the context of the particular ecology of the site, to the economy of the site, to the design's program, and above all to the problem being solved. The designer also has a responsibility to use materials and species that are available."

Lee F. Mindel, AIA, left, and Peter Shelton with their Window Chairs, designed with beechwood frames in 1988 and manufactured today by The Manheim Companies.

Arboretum Collection *designed by Shelton Mindel & Associates for Jack Lenor Larsen, including: Linden bench, 1990, with ebonized legs; Boxwood Ottoman, 1991, with mahogany legs; Linden Daybed, 1990, with mahogany legs; Alderbrook Sofa, 1990, with mahogany legs; and Hawthorne Chairs, 1992, with maple legs. Photography by Lizzie Himmel*

BEDS

Margaret-Lindsay Holton

Clodagh

Garouste & Bonetti

Agnes Bourne

Raul Velayos

Borek Sípek

Mimi London

Paolo Favoretto

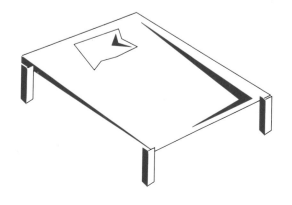

Gianfranco Frattini

William T. Georgis

Cannon / Bullock

Dakota Jackson

Gandy / Peace, Inc.

Antonio ("Budji") Layug

Juan Montoya

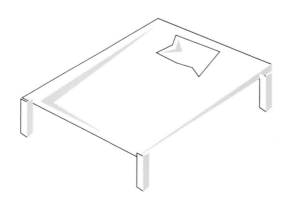

Margaret-Lindsay Holton

A client recently called Margaret-Lindsay Holton "the Linley of the North," and her work certainly has many aspects in common with the British cabinetmaker David Linley. Everything she has done since she, just one year out of college, sold her Lindsay typeface to Letraset, speaks of her originality, fine craftsmanship and reverence for detail.

Lindsay, now headquartered in Toronto, learned fine furniture making from her cabinetmaker father. She started receiving awards and being invited to exhibit just four years after she established her own firm, M.L.H. Productions, in 1986. Clients of her restoration abilities include Sotheby's of Canada, Rochelle & Co., William IV and Co., and the Royal Ontario Museum. Among her recent private commissions have been the restoration of six museum-quality Burmese rosewood antique tables, and the restoration of an 1870 English chest-on-chest of burled walnut. Yet she is mostly known for designing unique one-of-a-kind wood interiors. The motifs can vary from Islamic-Turkish to Japanese to Shaker. It is from this vantage point as furniture designer that she is often invited into the realm of architecture and interior design by her clients.

PHOTOGRAPHY COURTESY OF MARGARET-LINDSAY HOLTON

"I operate by the simple maxim: 'Live the ordinary life in a non-ordinary way.' In the design of my furniture I am often asked to create the entire 'set.' I attempt to quickly discern the stylistic boundaries of my clients' worldly ambitions and dreams. From that moment on I keep a notebook of ideas—thumbnail sketches and thoughts that amplify the various moods and feelings of my discoveries. Then, for the clients, I proceed to the presentation drawings and mock-ups. I respond to the clients' requests as a thoroughbred to a bridle-bit. The object is always to win the race and this demands strength, speed, stamina and, surprisingly, wit. Like a court jester, I have to encourage them to feel free to enjoy both the function and the fantasy of the pleasant material obstacle course I have laid in their way."

"The design, fabrication and function of fine furniture are irrefutably bound together. Weaken one aspect and you weaken the whole. Fine furniture, by definition, must function; it must be soundly made by an experienced craftsperson; and it must be pleasing to the evolving cultural eye. To slip off in one area can ruin the work, but, more importantly, it will not only fail the needs of the client, it will demolish the reputation of the designer."

"All designers (artists), in whatever discipline, must articulate, to the best of their abilities, their appreciation, respect and understanding of how to live in harmony with the wondrous forces of Nature. We have been provided with a superabundance of raw materials. Living in a cave is, fundamentally, no different from living in a condo. How we choose to live is another question. We can choose to live as beasts, or as noble creatures. I think it is my duty to honor the noble."

Rosedale Manor Bed. *Designed by Margaret-Lindsay Holton, 1991. Solid mahogany. Through M.L.H. Productions.*

"Quality never goes out of fashion. The design is deceptive. Initially it looks like a traditional four-poster bed. All the detailing and the French-polish finishing would, to an inexperienced eye, indicate that the bed is a well-built museum-quality antique. But make no mistake, this is a 'modern' bed. By fusing various woodworking trends of both the eighteenth and nineteenth centuries I have designed a 'Georgian Federal Upper-Canadian' solid mahogany four-poster with rare chamfered posts and a uniquely stylized acorn finial."

—*Margaret-Lindsay Holton*

Photography by Toni Hafkensheid

Children's Beds. *Designed by Margaret-
Lindsay Holton, 1990 (twin beds) and
1993 (double bed). The twins are solid
cherry wood. The double bed is maple.
One-of-a-kind designs through M.L.H.
Productions.*

*"A bed of one's own is probably the
most sacred of individual spaces. Not only
is it a place for rest and relaxation, but
also it can be the venue of great thought
and spiraling ambition. The twin beds
were designed for two brothers with totems
of animal power distinct to each. To
heighten their sense of privacy, I designed
the beds at an uncommonly high level of
30 inches. The older boy is the loner, the
owl. The second son is bouncy and bois-
terous, a doer...ergo, the bear motif.*

*"For the daughter, whose double bed
is shown here, something else was needed
altogether. I was adamant that she be surrounded by visual details that would
enhance her sense of beauty, grace and
refinement—thus the delicately hand-
carved frieze of overhanging maple
branches. Inside, on the footboard facing
her, is another hand-carved frieze of wild
roses, hummingbirds and dragonflies. If
she ever has a daughter, it is likely that this
bed will be passed on to her."*

—Margaret-Lindsay Holton
Photography by Toni Hafkensheid

Clodagh

*C*lodagh's innovative work employs a holistic approach to design integrating architecture, finishes, furnishings and landscaping. Her bold use of natural materials and exploitation of the unexpected are equally represented in the Dentsu Presentation Center in Tokyo, a sprawling penthouse in Manhattan, and a chair. Employing a depth of European influences, as well as an expanding pool of American artisans, she has achieved a signature look.

At seventeen, Clodagh was Ireland's hottest fashion designer. Moving to Spain, she designed environmentally conscious housing, reflecting ancient Moorish building techniques and employing solar and wind energy. Now headquartered in New York City, Clodagh has founded several companies: Clodagh Design International, a design studio for residential and commercial projects; Clodagh Design Works, focusing on furniture and accessories; and The Center for American Design, a retail and wholesale center for jewelry, furniture and home accessories in the Soho area of New York City. Clodagh's iconoclastic motto is "Why not!"

"Being a designer who works in architectural, interior, furniture and product design and gardens allows cross fertilization from all these disciplines and allows a macro view as well as a micro view of each project."

"Unless a design functions, the piece becomes yet another object—so function and, if possible, multi-function, drive all my design."

"The designer's responsibility is to strive for the highest percentage of perfection in all areas through design and specifications based on careful research."

Harwood Bed. *Designed by Clodagh, 1989. Stepped reeded uprights of copper with integral bud vases at the foot of the bed. Through Clodagh Design Works. Photography by Daniel Aubry*

Flug Bed. *Designed by Clodagh, 1993. Patinated bronze and wood. The four posters support a delicate bronze canopy and are topped with lighted torchieres. Custom reading lamps by Daniel Berglund are collared on to the two head posters. The headboard runs the full height of the bed for comfortable reading and relaxing. Through Clodagh Design Works. Photography by Daniel Aubry*

Garouste & Bonetti   Elizabeth Garouste ◇ Mattia Bonetti

Parisian designers Elizabeth Garouste and Mattia Bonetti offer welcome surprises throughout their design. In their furniture they reflect on a number of subjects, from skyscrapers to ballerinas, then translate their visions into functional objects composed of fine woods, carefully wrought metals, fascinating patinas, an edited collection of sumptuous fabrics, as well as terra-cotta and papier-mâché.

Garouste and Bonetti exhibited their first collection of furniture and objects in 1981 at Jansen's in Paris. Soon they became the "leaders" in the "barbarian" and "baroque" styles which were copiously and internationally adopted by the media. They have taken part in many group exhibitions in various museums, including: Museo di Milano; Cooper-Hewitt, New York; Seibu, Tokyo; Victoria and Albert, London; Centre Georges Pompidou, Paris.

At the request of public and private enterprises, Garouste and Bonetti created a pedestrian bridge in Quimper, France; a set of furniture for the Ministry of Culture in Paris; the Haute-Couture showrooms as well as the international boutiques for couturier Christian Lacroix; the offices of the Banque Bruxelles-Lambert in Geneva; and the hall and restaurant of the castle Museum of Regensburg, Germany.

"When we intervene on architecture or decoration, we always have the desire of harmony or antagonism or something else. It depends. But in any case we always take care of the function of the rooms and the personality of our client."

"The design and its fabrication and its function are equally important and should generally be associated and interdependent."

"The responsibility of the designer is to be fair with his own ideas."

__Tormina__. Designed by Garouste & Bonetti, 1992. Patina wrought iron, silver-plated bronze, and silk. An edition of eight. Available through Neotu, New York and Paris.
Photography courtesy of Neotu

Agnes Bourne

*T*o frolic through Agnes Bourne's design studio and furniture show-room in San Francisco is like going on a picnic—so filled are they with joyous odes to living through design. So it was no surprise when she created a bed whose poplar columns and hand-wrought iron branches actually look just like an ideal setting for a picnic.

Bourne studied art and architecture in Florence, Italy, and received her Bachelor of Arts degree from Mills College in Studio Art and Art History. She did post-graduate work at the University of Pennsylvania in American Studies and Architecture and also earned a Certificate of Design from the Rudolph Schaeffer School of Design, San Francisco.

She has been involved in the practice of design for twenty years. In 1987 she introduced her own line of furniture, The Agnes Bourne Collection, and has since expanded the Agnes Bourne Showroom to include the work of furniture artists and selected manufactured furniture, fabric and lighting lines.

"Being an interior designer affects my perspective as a furniture designer by making me look at each piece as it relates to another and its environment. I am very aware of relationships of shapes in space and interaction of objects and humans. Spaces can empower people to be as magnificent as they can be and furniture enhances that support."

"The design is most important. The quality of a product is part of the design. Good design, good workmanship, good function are all integrated and inseparable. Poorly made things—no matter how clever the design—have no merit. Likewise, functionless well-made objects are of little use."

"Designers create access for people to reach their highest potential. Designers are the translators of technology and philosophy into livable space and a sustainable planet. Designers have the tools to transform the physical world to meet the needs of people while preserving the earth. They are the key to longevity, ecology and economy."

Picnic Bed*. Designed by Agnes Bourne, 1991. Manufactured and represented by Agnes Bourne, Inc. Poplar columns with hand-wrought iron branches. Custom sizes available besides the standard King, Queen and Full. Headboard, base and two pillows upholstered in Agnes Bourne Fabrics or custom.*
Photography by Jock McDonald

Raul Velayos

*T*o Raul Velayos of Fort Lauderdale, Florida, being an interior designer does not have a profound impact on his art, in this case his furniture design.

"When I work in home design, I am creating an image from components which, when put together in a certain fashion, provoke a special feeling. But when I design furniture, I am expressing an artistic idea," says the Peruvian-born Velayos who, feeling unfulfilled after years as an interior

designer, found that, for him, painting and furniture design offered greater satisfaction. "I needed to be able to express myself rather than try to influence the taste of others," says Velayos, whose paintings have since been displayed at the Fort Lauderdale Contemporary Museum of Art on three occasions.

His signature furniture, with every part of every piece handcrafted and personally supervised by Velayos himself, is garnering an equally appreciative audience among residential clients who view the rooms in their homes as art.

"When I design furniture, I also am expressing an artistic idea. That is why, for me, the design is the driving force. Of course, a piece must be very well made. If a piece is poorly constructed, its value is diminished the moment it begins to deteriorate. The fact that my furniture is functional allows me to enjoy the benefits of commercial success. Each piece, however, exists and is produced for its artistic value."

"Furniture designers have different responsibilities depending on why they design and what type of furniture they design. For me, furniture should be timeless. It should be appreciated the moment it is finished, two years later, and one hundred years after that. This concept is a very important part of my artistic perspective. My furniture is basically simple. It can be appreciated when placed among other pieces which are not similar, as part of an eclectic setting. Each piece is an individual work of art."

Raul Velayos surrounded by three other pieces from the same collection, these including ¾ inch thick bronze forming a grid for the doors on the vertical cabinets supporting the secretary, the bottom shelf of the end table (at left), and the bottom shelves of his stackable, marble-topped shelving units.
Photography by Myro Rosky

Queen-size bed. *Designed by Raul Velayos, 1992. Fabricated under the personal direction of the designer and with the support of Janet Varga. Hammered alder wood finished with oil and wax, combined with hand-crafted and hammered ¾ inch thick bronze which is treated with acid. Available through the designer in any size. From a fifteen-piece collection, which includes consoles, tables, chests and open cabinetry, in which each piece incorporates the designer's inlaid bronze "V" signature. Photography by Myro Rosky*

Borek Sípek

*B*orn in Prague, Borek Sípek opened his architecture and design studio in Amsterdam in 1983. Before and since, his commissions and awards have been many, including the appointment, as Court Architect for the Czech Republic, by President Vaclav Havel, and La Croix Chevalier dans l'Ordre des Arts et des Lettres by the French government. He also has continued to be active in education, at various times serving as lecturer in architecture and design theory. Yet when it comes to theorizing about his own design, his statements are short, direct, and to the point.

His work is in the collections of the Museum of Modern Art in New York, Museum for Decorative Art in Prague, Kunstmuseum in Düsseldorf, Stedelijk Museum in Amsterdam, Museum Boymans-van Beuningen in Rotterdam, Museum for Decorative Arts in Lyon and Paris, The Corning Museum of Glass in New York, The Hague Municipal Museum, Design Museum in London, Vitra Design Museum in Weil am Rhein, and Denver Art Museum.

On his design philosophy: "Art is without philosophy."

On the influence of his background in architecture and interior design on his furniture design: "In my view, furniture is part of design."

On the order of importance of the various aspects of furniture design: "The design itself implies the fabrication and the function."

On the designer's responsibility: "To give culture to the people."

***Bed**. Designed by Borek Sípek, 1991. Wood and linen. One prototype and one final example. No longer available. Photography by León Gulikers*

Mimi London

A protégé of the late Michael Taylor, Mimi London also is known for her similar emphasis on comfort, use of natural fibers and products, and incorporation of the outside into the interior of a space. In fact, even

PHOTOGRAPHY BY TODD GRAY

if you didn't know who "invented" log and tree-trunk furniture, you would probably guess that it was London, and you would be right.

She began her career designing furniture as well as interiors, and opened her own showroom in the mid-1970s. Now located in Los Angeles at the Pacific Design Center, she has a staff of ten who help her carry forth some six to twelve interior projects a year as well as new furnishings ideas.

"Being an interior designer gives me a sense of appropriate scale and of what is possible when it comes to designing furniture. The more one knows about how a room goes together, the more one's designs can work with other people's work."

"In terms of priorities, function takes precedence. If it doesn't work right, forget it. Second is fabrication, which to me is synonymous with quality. Lastly, design comes into play. There is so little original work done that originality does get clients' attention—and captures their imagination."

"Ergonomics is such a distancing word. I prefer to try to make my clients comfortable."

Bed. *Designed by Mimi London, 1986. Manufactured by Mimi London. Montana birch trees. The tables are from Mimi London's Montana spruce collection.*
Photography by Jim McHugh

Paolo Favaretto

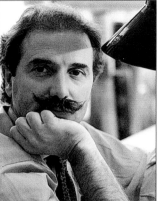

*S*ince 1973, when he was still studying architecture in Venezia, Paolo Favaretto has had his own professional practice in industrial design and corporate identity, headquartered in the city where he was born, Padova. Always attentive to the problems of production and always working in close contact with the technical offices of the company with whom he is associated, he has achieved much experience in the use of a wide variety of materials and in different sectors of design. His works, for which he has received numerous distinctions, often incorporate a high level of technology and include orthodontist equipment (patient chair and work station), multi-adjustable task and operative office seating, electric plugs and televisions. He also designs furniture and lighting fixtures for the home.

"I think having an architectural background helps one to approach furniture design problems not only from a technical point of view or according to the marketing policy of the moment. Being an architect helps one also to take into consideration the cultural and social environment and background in which and for which we are working and operating."

"In considering the importance of design, fabrication or function in furniture design, I would certainly put function in first place. I would say that fabrication comes next as far as the quality/price relationship is concerned. In fact, a good product at a competitive price can reach quite a wide range of the public."

"Ergonomics, ecology, longevity—all the three together and many more are the designer's responsibility. Also it is important to guide and improve people's tastes by offering products of clean and simple design."

Placido. Designed by Paolo Favaretto, 1991. Manufactured by Estel spa. Walnut and lacquer. Collection includes: bed, chest of drawers, bedside table. Photography courtesy of Estel

Gianfranco Frattini

*G*ianfranco Frattini was born in Padova in 1926, took a degree in Architecture at the Polytechnic of Milan in 1953. Today he lives and works in Milan dedicating his professional activity mainly to architecture, interior design and industrial design.

He was mentioned for honors for the Compasso Golden Prize many times, as well as the "Triennali" of Milan.

Besides the "Triennali," his participation in showrooms and exhibitions has been extensive, including the International Fair of Paris, the International Fair of Cologne, the Euroluce and the ICSID Exhibition of Milan.

In the area of industrial design he collaborates with Acerbis International, Arteluce, Artemide, Bernini, Casigliani, Cassina, Fantoni, Fusital, ICF, Lema, Lucitalia, Mazzei, Mobileffe, Progetti, Knoll International and Kron.

His products are exhibited permanently in the design sector of the Museum of Modern Art, New York; Museum of Contemporary Art, Chicago; and the Die Neue Sammlung Staaliches Museum fur angewandte Kunst Munchen.

PHOTOGRAPHY BY STUDIO AZZURRO FOTOGRAFIA

"Without doubt, to be an architect and an interior designer has been and is still now fundamental for my profession, especially because there is a tight relation between architectural project and furniture design."

"In my opinion, the study of the function conditions both fabrication and design."

"The responsibility of the designer must cover every aspect of the project's process."

I Bagatti Bed. *Designed by Gianfranco Frattini, 1987. Manufactured by Fantoni Arredamenti-Osoppo. Wooden bed with headboard and resting pillows made of leather.*
Photography by Studio Conti-Udine/Agenzia Varotto-Padova

William T. Georgis

Working as an architect since 1983, William T. Georgis has designed and completed residential, institutional and commercial projects including a *pied-à-terre* at the Carlyle Hotel, a Fifth Avenue apartment, the lobby of a cooperative apartment building and a residence in Michigan. Currently he is working on renovations to the Holly Solomon Gallery in Manhattan, additions to a house in Croton-on-Hudson, the renovation and decoration of a North Kale Shore Drive apartment in Chicago, and furnishings for a residence in Brooklyn, New York.

Prior to establishing his own firm in 1992, Georgis worked for Robert Venturi of Venturi, Rauch and Scott Brown in 1983 and from 1984-1992 for Robert A. M. Stern for whom he designed the winning entry in 1988 for the Norman Rockwell Museum at Stockbridge, which he supervised to completion. He is also responsible for the design of the Roger Tory

Peterson Institute in Jamestown, New York, which is currently under construction.

Also for Robert A. M. Stern, Georgis has supervised the design of decorative arts for the Parrish museum at Southampton, New York; Martex; Hickory Business Furniture; Swid Powell; Munari Design Associati; and Baldinger Architectural Lighting. His work has been exhibited at the National Academy of Design and at Columbia University, and is part of the permanent collections of the Metropolitan Museum of Art in New York City, The Art Institute of Chicago, and the Denver Art Museum.

Georgis received a Bachelor of Arts degree from Stanford University in 1980, and a Master of Architecture degree from Princeton University in 1983.

"Designing furniture enables the architect to shift from large to small scale. I consider this a special opportunity, as often the grand scale of architecture informs pieces of furniture. I often conceive of furniture as a miniaturization of architecture, utilizing the same rules of composition, order and balance. Furniture, because of its particular construction and function, allows a very different mode of expression to prevail. In particular, furniture design encourages a more private and personal and sometimes humorous expression to influence design."

"It is impossible to stratify the importance of design, fabrication and function in furniture. In the best pieces of furniture all three are harmoniously balanced."

"The responsibility of the designer varies depending on the user. In the design of custom residential furniture, comfort and function are always important. Economics often have less to do with the design than the client's dreams and aspirations."

Beds for the I. B. Dweck Residence, New York City. Designed by William T. Georgis, 1993. Fabricated by Volz, Clark & Associates. Swiss pearwood, curly maple, water gilding, cotton velvet. Photography by Kevin Downey

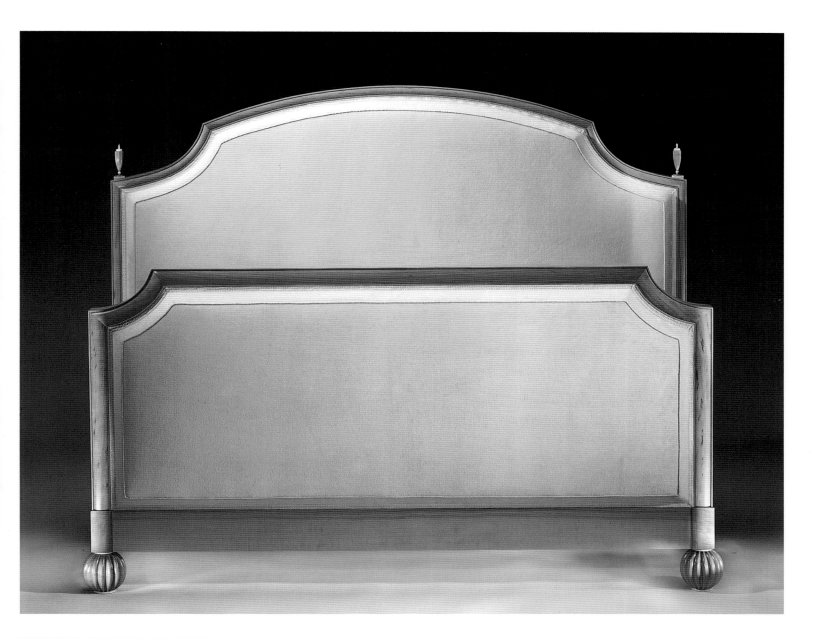

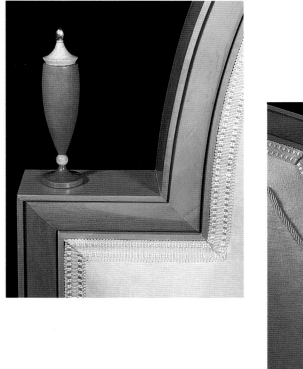

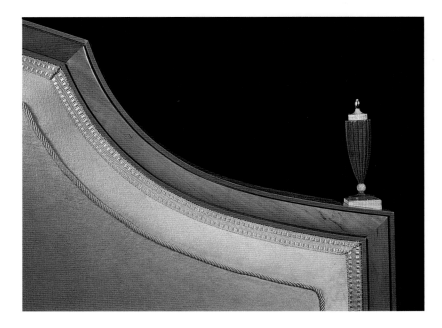

Cannon/Bullock   Richard Cannon • Richard Bullock

"With my partner Richard Bullock (left) being an interior designer as well as product designer, and with myself being an architect and interior designer, we tend to think of a piece of furniture as part of the total environment, not as an object by itself," says Richard Cannon (right) of Cannon/Bullock, Los Angeles. "We view each piece as helping to define a space. A piece of furniture has the same role as a wall or a ceiling in that it must perform a function and, in so doing, it contributes to an overall atmosphere, evoking an emotional and physical response from human inhabitants."

Cannon and Bullock, who create products for other designers as well as for their own interiors projects, also run a showroom for the products and services of other designers, artists and craftsmen. The general tendency among those represented by Cannon and Bullock as well in their own work is the use of rich and dramatic finishes and details and a great sense of mood. Yet they say that their first and foremost concern when designing is function.

"Function must be served well and logically. If an element in a space does not function properly, it should be removed. Only after function is addressed, and this includes quality fabrication, should one consider how an element contributes to the overall atmosphere of a space. Here the role should be defined by the designer: Is it a part of the choir? Does it have a solo? Is it the star or co-star? The designer must sort this out in composing the space."

"The designer must look at the assignment and respond logically. The assignment may be to create a room that will endure a lifetime, or it may be to create 'a night to remember.' It's the assignment that dictates materials and budget."

Campaign Bed. *Designed and manufactured by Cannon/Bullock, 1993. Silver leafed wood frame. Bedding from Cannon/Bullock Custom Services includes a cotton sateen fabric from the designers' Doge's Palace Collection of papers and fabrics. The Harlequin patterned wall of silver leaf on a flat paint surface is also from Cannon/Bullock Custom Services. The side tables are from Niedermeier; the pen and ink sketch on rice paper is by Richard Cannon. Photography by Jerome Adamstein*

Dakota Jackson

Dakota Jackson's previous career on the stage, first as magician and then as a postmodern dancer, caused him to invest his early furniture with an air of mystery and theatricality that can be seen in his designs today. Twenty years later, as creative head of his namesake company in New York City that produces furniture suitable for residential, office, and public spaces, he still is known for innovative pieces that are as visually striking as they are comfortable.

The Big Sleep Collection won accolades at the 1993 International Contemporary Furniture Fair and the ICFF Critics' Award for "Best Body of Work."

Dakota Jackson furniture is in many museum collections, including: the American Craft Museum, New York; The Brooklyn Museum, New York; Cooper-Hewitt Museum, New York; and Design Museum, London.

"My first calling was as a designer and maker of furniture, then expanding into interior space design and now we are architects. So my first interest has always been rooted in furniture. As a designer of interior spaces in the '70s, I did the opposite of what architects might do—they made furniture as extensions of the architecture, or designed 'built-ins.' I would 'build out.' I would approach a room as if the entire space were a single piece of furniture, and then play out the specific features of that furniture, building out from the walls into the center of the room. The furniture would, in a sense, become the architecture."

"At this point in my career, I see no separation between furniture design, its fabrication and its function. As furniture styles changed from the '60s through the '90s, and my career matured along with them, the issues I chose to express as a designer have likewise shifted. At a certain time the issue was to challenge the nature of function itself. At another time I wanted to redefine the meaning of the fine object and the materials that contributed to it. Another time saw me exploring furniture's relationship to craft. And there was the element of magic, from my prior career as a magician, and what that might add to the meaning of the object: a layer of mystery, surprise or infinite possibility.

"My more recent concerns are about the totality of the well-designed object: it has to be extraordinarily well made, expressing recognizable elements of fine craftsmanship; it should challenge our sense of aesthetics; and it must function properly."

The Big Sleep. Designed by Dakota Jackson, 1993. Manufactured by Dakota Jackson, Inc. Beds and case goods of ash in a variety of stains. Includes king and queen size beds, daybed, sleigh bed, armoire, night table available in a variety of configurations, mirror, and bureau available as highboy and lowboy. Photography by Steve Tague

Gandy/Peace, Inc.   Charles D. Gandy · William B. Peace

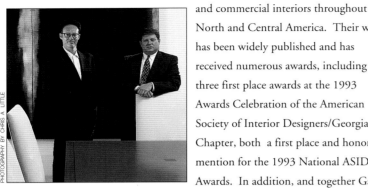

Gandy/Peace, Inc. is a multi-disciplined, internationally recognized and award-winning design firm based in Atlanta, Georgia. Charles Gandy, FASID, IBD, and his partner William B. Peace, create residential and commercial interiors throughout North and Central America. Their work has been widely published and has received numerous awards, including three first place awards at the 1993 Awards Celebration of the American Society of Interior Designers/Georgia Chapter, both a first place and honorable mention for the 1993 National ASID Awards. In addition, and together Gandy and Peace received the 1993 Southeastern Designer of the Year by ADAC (Atlanta Decorative Arts Center).

"Our role as interior designers affords us the opportunity to understand interior space and its relationship to the objects, be they furniture or people, within the space. We understand human scale as well as the human psyche. Thus, as furniture designers we have a broader vision of the impact of finished pieces both from a practical as well as psychological viewpoint."

"What's the most important—design, fabrication or function? The answer is simple: all three. We are constantly dwelling on QUALITY...quality of the 'real' and quality of the 'abstract.' When focusing on the quality of the 'real' we ask 'Is this the best wood?...the best hinge?...the best craftsmanship? Likewise, although sometimes harder to define, we are interested in the quality of the abstract: the scale!, the proportion!, the line!, the rhythm!, and all the many other intangible elements that determine a 'quality' design over a lesser one. We are concerned about 'connection'...how one material meets another...how the piece actually goes together. Throughout this quest for quality we keep a steadfast eye on the intended end use of our furniture. This means looking beyond the mere 'function' of the piece in specific terms to the 'status' of the piece within its setting. When successful, what appears to be the simplest piece of furniture is indeed quite complex."

*"In our opinion, it is the responsibility of the designer that his or her work be **appropriate**. That's a big word that demands incredible responsibility. To be sure, as designers, we must respect our environment and only design and specify products and materials that will maintain the ecological balances necessary to promote a quality life for humankind. Health, safety and welfare issues should always override aesthetic ones."*

Built-in Headboard. *Designed by Gandy/Peace, Inc., 1991. Pearl movinga wood in combination with stainless steel inlays. Custom design available through the designers.*

Designed to accommodate "his and hers" books, phones, clocks and other bedside necessities in a manner that would provide easy access but would simultaneously hide them from view. The exotic wood is quietly but classically handled. The subtle diamond pattern of the cabinetry is repeated in the tailored bedspread and bolster and complements the elegant, padded ebony horsehair wall. Photography by Chris A. Little

Rosewood and Cherry Headboard. *Designed by Gandy/Peace, Inc., 1990. Custom design available through the designers.*

The designers' concept for remodeling a very old and very traditional house was to pay homage to the old while simultaneously celebrating the new. This headboard, designed for the master bedroom, summarizes the entire project in one piece of furniture. Existing dark rosewood cabinets and shelving had to remain; however, in the re-work cherry became the wood of choice. The headboard, with its pediment shape and tall posts, although predominately made of cherry, is banded in rosewood. The traditional shapes are executed in contemporary details.
Photography by Tommy Thompson

Antonio ("Budji") Layug

Antonio ("Budji") Layug was born the third of eight children to a prominent Filipino manufacturing family. While showing his interest in design from an early age, Budji went on to study design at the New York School of Interior Design and architecture at the University Santo Thomas in Manila.

Budji's original furniture line was first seen in America at Bloomingdale's New York in 1981 and featured a year later in Bloomingdale's Philippine Exhibit. He built his own factory in Batangas in order to custom build his "Giant Bamboo" furniture. His showroom openings followed…Los Angeles in 1984…San Francisco in 1985…then Seattle, Boston, Boynton Beach (Florida), Phoenix, Singapore, Milan….and his interior design business continued to prosper.

Budji was the winner of the prestigious American Merchandising Corporation Award for Design Excellence in 1984 and was recently the consulting designer to the 1993 Manila F.A.M.E. show. Though international in scope, Budji remains firmly rooted in his native Philippines, while his furniture designs and interior design work are evident from Milan to Tokyo to America and throughout the Pacific Rim.

Budji has said that designers frequently cannot understand the organic use of Pacific Rim raw materials because they do not live with them. He has very much lived with his medium and says: "I like to live with what is outside by bringing it into the living space. I enjoy melding high-tech rooms with organic materials, antiques with contemporary settings, mixing cultures and designs…."

"As an architect and designer, I think a feeling for the space is very important and a total designer approach from exterior to interior is essential to creating a style that will endure the passage of time. This includes the home furnishings and furniture designs that complement the space."

"The totality of the whole process is enjoyable and important. The design and function of it are only the result of the conceptualization of an idea from abstract to reality, from raw material to functional designs."

"The most important responsibility of today's designer is to interpret a style or designs for contemporary living that will represent to future generations how society or people lived with art during his lifetime."

Twin-Size Opium Couch. *Designed by Antonio ("Budji") Layug, 1982. Giant Bamboo, natural finish. Seat cushion and five pillows. Available through The Budji Collections, Inc.*
Photography courtesy of Budji Layug Designs

Twin-Size Opium Couch Bed.
Designed by Antonio ("Budji") Layug, 1982. Available through The Budji Collections, Inc. Giant Bamboo, natural finish. Shown with Wilo Occasional Chair and Ottoman in stretched leather and rattan, Halfmoon Sofa in Giant Bamboo, Cluster Curved Giant Bamboo Side Table, Giant Bamboo Tripod Coffee Table. All from The Budji Collections, Inc.
Photography courtesy of Budji Layug Designs

Juan Montoya

*F*or Juan Montoya, interiors are a careful balance of color and space. His rooms tend to be monochromatic with objects playing a large part in the color and design statement. Attention to shadows, size, spatial quality and textures is his hallmark. He favors abstract design, but also that which shows both refinement and simplicity.

"A room does not need to be filled," he says. "Rather I look at the room to see what it has to offer and what I can do to enhance it. Often, it's more important to look at the 'shell' of the room, because the 'shell' dictates finally how the room will be designed. Also, eccentricity is always preferable to the bland and the safe."

Montoya, born in Bogota, Colombia, is president of Juan Montoya Design Corporation, New York City, which he founded in 1978, and he is also president of Juan Montoya Furniture & Accessories, which he founded in 1988.

"Being an interior designer and being a furniture designer are very much part of the same item, since you can't take one from the other. Scale is the essence of design, and architecture is all about scale. Therefore, the proportion of a chair relates directly to the scale of a room."

"Function comes first. From there the style or design of the piece of furniture is derived. Then comes the fabrication."

"The greatest responsibility of the designer? Ergonomics!"

Bed. *Designed by Juan Montoya, 1993. Wrought iron. Manufactured for Portobelo Collection. Shown with other Montoya designs: a wrought iron standing lamp and black lacquered wood shoji screen manufactured for Portobelo Collection; and a table, bust and vase available through Juan Montoya Furniture and Accessories. Photography courtesy of Juan Montoya Design Corporation*

Appendix

Architects and Designers

United States

Milo Baughman
Milo Baughman Design Inc.
132 E Street, Suite 1
Salt Lake City, Utah 84103
Tel: (801) 539-0448
Fax: (801) 539-0451

Ward Bennett
One West 72nd Street, Penthouse A
New York, New York 10023
Tel: (212) 580-1358

Samuel Botero
Samuel Botero Associates, Inc.
150 East 58th Street
New York, New York 10155
Tel: (212) 935-5155
Fax: (212) 832-0714

Lisa Bottom
Bottom Duvivier
2603 Broadway
Redwood City, California 94063
Tel: (415) 361-1209
Fax: (415) 361-1229

Agnes Bourne
Agnes Bourne, Inc.
Showplace Design Center
Two Henry Adams Street, Showroom 220
San Francisco, California 94103
Tel: (415) 626-6883
Fax: (415) 626-2489

Cannon/Bullock
(Richard Cannon, ISID, and
Richard Bullock)
8407 Melrose Place
Los Angeles, California 90069
Tel: (213) 651-2875
Fax: (213) 651-2876 (call first)

Steve Chase
Steve Chase Associates
70-005 39th Avenue
Rancho Mirage, California 92270
Tel: (619) 324-4602
Fax: (619) 328-3006

Laurie Ann Clemans
Laurie Ann Clemans Design
1248 Homestead Avenue
Walnut Creek, California 94598
Tel/Fax: (510) 938-3224

Clodagh
Clodagh Design International
365 First Avenue
New York, New York 10010
Tel: (212) 673-9202
Fax: (212) 614-9125

Coop Himmelblau
(Wolf D. Prix and Helmut Swiczinsky)
8561 Hihuera Street
Culver City, California 90232
Tel: (310) 838-8264
Fax: (310) 838-8267
[See also *Austria*]

Timothy deFiebre, vice president
International Contract Furnishings, Inc.
10 Maple Street
Norwood, New Jersey 07648
Tel: (201) 784-0200
Fax: (201) 784-8209

Alfredo De Vido; FAIA
Alfredo De Vido Associates
1044 Madison Avenue
New York, New York 10021
Tel: (212) 517-6100
Fax: (212) 517-6103

Rand Elliott, AIA
Elliott + Associates Architects
6709 North Classen, Suite 101
Oklahoma City, Oklahoma 73116
Tel: (405) 843-9554
Fax: (405) 843-9607

Ergo Design Works Inc.
(Lory Johansson and June Robinson)
8112½ West Third Street, Suite D
Los Angeles, California 90048
Tel: (213) 658-8901
Fax: (213) 658-8903

Heather Faulding, AIA
Faulding Associates
420 West 24th Street
New York, New York 10011
Tel: (212) 366-1711
Fax: (212) 366-1715

Janice Feldman
JANUS et Cie
Pacific Design Center, B-146
8687 Melrose Avenue
Los Angeles, California 90069
Tel: (310) 652-7090
Fax: (310) 652-7928

Gandy/Peace, Inc.
(Charles D. Gandy, FASID, IBD, and
William B. Peace)
3195 Paces Ferry Place, Northwest
Atlanta, Georgia 30305-1307
Tel: (404) 237-8681
Fax: (404) 237-6150

Robert Garcia
Therien & Co., Inc.
411 Vermont Street
San Francisco, California 94107
Tel: (415) 956-8850
Fax: (415) 861-2192
also
716 North La Cienega Boulevard
Los Angeles, California 90069
Tel: (310) 657-4615
Fax: (310) 657-2819

Frank O. Gehry, FAIA
Frank O. Gehry & Associates, Inc.
1520-B Cloverfield Boulevard
Santa Monica, California 90404
Tel: (310) 828-6088
Fax: (310) 828-2098

William T. Georgis
41 Fifth Avenue
New York, New York 10003
Tel: (212) 529-5153
Fax: (212) 529-5258

Goodman Charlton
(Jeffrey Goodman and Steven Charlton)
1500 Rising Glen Road
Los Angeles, California 90069
Tel: (310) 657-7069
Fax: (310) 657-1868

Goralnick ⋆ Buchanan A&D, Inc.
(Barry Goralnick and Michael Buchanan)
2109 Broadway, Suite 1492
New York, New York 10023-2130
Tel: (212) 362-7217
Fax: (212) 362-7254

Michael Graves
Michael Graves, Architect
341 Nassau Street
Princeton, New Jersey 08540
Tel: (609) 924-6409
Fax: (609) 924-1795

Paul Haigh, BA (Hons), M.DesRCA, AIA
Haigh Architects Designers
63 Pemberwick Road
Greenwich, Connecticut 06831
Tel: (203) 532-0201
Fax: (203) 532-0205

Jean-Pierre Heim, Architecte D.P.L.G.
Jean-Pierre Heim & Associates and
Design Connection International
140 West 69th Street, 46B
New York, New York 10023
Tel: (212) 724-7132
Fax: (212) 724-7943
[See also *France*]

Thomas A. Heinz
Heinz & Co. of Illinois, Inc.
120 Callan Avenue
Evanston, Illinois 60202
Tel/Fax: (708) 328-6552

Margaret Helfand
Margaret Helfand Architects
32 East 38th Street
New York, New York 10016
Tel: (212) 779-7260
Fax: (212) 779-7758

Richard Himmel, FASID
Lubliner and Himmel Corporation
1729 Merchandise Mart Plaza
Chicago, Illinois 60654
Tel: (312) 527-5700
Fax: (312) 527-2169

Thayer Hopkins
Thayer Hopkins Architect
1129 Kansas Street
San Francisco, California 94107
Tel: (415) 434-0320
Fax: (415) 434-2409

John Hutton
Donghia Furniture & Textiles
485 Broadway
New York, New York 10013
Tel: (212) 925-2777
Fax: (212) 925-4819

Dakota Jackson
Dakota Jackson, Inc.
306 East 61st Street
New York, New York 10021
Tel: (212) 838-9444
Fax: (212) 758-6413

Ronn Jaffe, ASID, IBD
Ronn Jaffe Incorporated
The Design Studio Building
9204 Harrington Drive
Potomac, Maryland 20854
Tel: (301) 365-3500
Fax: (301) 365-3157

Noel Jeffrey
Noel Jeffrey, Inc.
215 East 58th Street
New York, New York 10022
Tel: (212) 935-7775
Fax: (212) 935-8280

Dennis Jenkins
5813 Southwest 68th Street
South Miami, Florida 33143
Tel: (305) 665-6960
Fax: (305) 665-6971

James F. Jereb, Ph.D.
Tribal Design
1001 East Alameda
Santa Fe, New Mexico 87501
Tel: (505) 989-8765
Fax: (505) 989-3353

Scott Johnson, AIA
Johnson Fain and Pereira Associates
6100 Wilshire Boulevard, Fifth Floor
Los Angeles, California 90048
Tel: (213) 933-8341
Fax: (213) 933-3120

Elyse B. Lacher
Cy Mann International
305 East 63rd Street
New York, New York 10021
Tel: (212) 758-6830
Fax: (212) 758-6735

Leavitt/Weaver
(Craig Leavitt and Stephen Weaver)
451 Tully Road
Modesto, California 95350
Tel: (209) 521-5125
Fax: (209) 571-8340

Sally Sirkin Lewis
J. Robert Scott & Associates, Inc.
8727 Melrose Avenue
Los Angeles, California 90069
Tel: (310) 659-4910
Fax: (310) 659-4994

Mimi London
Pacific Design Center
8687 Melrose Avenue
Los Angeles, California 90069
Tel: (310) 855-2567
Fax: (310) 855-0213

Robert Frank McAlpine
Robert Frank McAlpine
Architecture, Inc.
Sabel Mansion
644 South Perry Street
Montgomery, Alabama 36104
Tel: (205) 262-8315
Fax: (205) 269-1637

Juan Montoya, ASID
Juan Montoya Design Corporation
80 Eighth Avenue
New York, New York 10011
Tel: (212) 242-3622
Fax: (212) 242-3743

Moore Andersson Architects
2102 Quarry Road
Austin, Texas 78703
Tel: (512) 476-5780
Fax: (512) 476-0858

Eric Owen Moss, FAIA
Eric Owen Moss Architects
8557 Higuera Street
Culver City, California 90232
Tel: (310) 839-1199
Fax: (310) 839-7922

Edward David Nieto, ISID
Edward David Nieto Design
Group, Inc.
108 North East 39th Street
Miami, Florida 33137
Tel: (305) 573-9555
Fax: (305) 573-2255

Sandra Nunnerly
Sandra Nunnerly, Inc.
112 East 71st Street
New York, New York 10021
Tel: (212) 472-9341
Fax: (212) 472-9346

José Luis Pérez Ortega
51 Richfield Street
Plainview, New York 11803
Tel: (516) 349-5932/34
[See also *Spain*]

Warren Platner, Architect
Warren Platner Associates Architects
18 Mitchell Drive
New Haven, Connecticut 06511
Tel: (203) 777-6471
Fax: (203) 562-4530

Bradley Rath
Studio Design Furniture
160 North Halsted Street, #2
Chicago, Illinois 60607
Tel: (312) 997-9900
Fax: (312) 243-6036

Charles A. Reimann
Reimann Mikami Inc.
560 North Nimitz Highway, Suite 206A
Honolulu, Hawaii 96817
Tel: (808) 538-6836
Fax: (808) 533-7589

Lauren Rottet, AIA
Keating-Mann-Jernigan-Rottet
606 South Olive
Los Angeles, California 90014
Tel: (213) 895-4700
Fax: (213) 895-4760

Geoffrey Scott, AIA
GSDA/Geoffrey Scott Design Associates
Post Office Box 554
Venice, California 90294
Tel/Fax: (310) 396-5416

Shelton Mindel & Associates
(Peter Shelton and Lee F. Mindel, AIA)
216 West 18th Street
New York, New York 10011
Tel: (212) 243-3939
Fax: (212) 727-7310

Harry Segil
8639 Venice Boulevard
Los Angeles, California 90034
Tel: (310) 559-7863
Fax: (310) 559-3387

Mark Simon, FAIA
Centerbrook Architects
Post Office Box 955
Essex, Connecticut 06426
Tel: (203) 767-0175
Fax: (203) 767-8719

Mark Singer
Mark Singer Designs
122 Powers Avenue
Santa Barbara, California 93103
Tel: (805) 963-2234
Fax: (805) 963-0028

Warren Snodgrass
Design Technology
2105 Shelter Bay
Mill Valley, California 94941
Tel: (415) 381-2353
Fax: (415) 381-4245

Dhana Solish, ASID Allied Member
424 Hilgard Avenue
Los Angeles, California 90024
Tel: (310) 474-3481
Fax: (310) 474-0198

Lenny Steinberg
Lenny Steinberg Design Associates
1802 Angelo Drive
Beverly Hills, California 90210
Tel/Fax: (310) 271-7870

Robert A.M. Stern, FAIA
Robert A.M. Stern Architects
211 West 61st Street
New York, New York 10023
Tel: (212) 246-1980
Fax: (212) 246-2486

Kipp Stewart
Post Office Drawer 6145
Carmel, California 93921
Tel: (408) 624-8969

Robert Stuffings
Robert Stuffings Associates
37 Osprey Point Drive
Osprey, Florida 34229
Tel/Fax: (813) 966-2400

Norman Sukkar
Norman Sukkar Furniture
13 Avenue A
New York, New York 10009
Tel: (212) 477-4477
Fax: (212) 260-1160

Stan Taylor
E.N.T Enterprises, Inc.
8479 Steeler Drive
Culver City, California 90232
Tel: (310) 202-6162
Fax: (310) 202-6706

Joseph Alcasar Terrell
Alcasar Terrell Environmental
    Design Group
119½ North Larchmont Boulevard
Los Angeles, California 90004
Tel: (213) 469-8044
Fax: (213) 469-0561

Adam Tihany
57 East 11th Street
New York, New York 10003
Tel: (212) 505-2360
Fax: (212) 529-3578

Larry Totah
Totah Design Inc.
654 North Larchmont Boulevard
Los Angeles, California 90004
Tel: (213) 467-2927
Fax: (213) 463-0377

Paul Tuttle
885 Toro Canyon Road
Montecito, California 93108
Tel: (805) 969-6026

Raul Velayos
820 Southeast Eighth Street
Fort Lauderdale, FL 33316
Tel: (305) 525-5343

Shepard Vineburg, ASID
Shepard Vineburg Design
4205 West 59th Street
Los Angeles, California 90043
Tel: (213) 295-8457
Fax: (213) 295-1395

Sherle Wagner
Sherle Wagner International, Inc.
60 East 57th Street
New York, New York 10022
Tel: (212) 758-3300
Fax: (212) 207-8010

Michael Wolk
Michael Wolk and Associates
2318 Northeast Second Court
Miami, Florida 33137
Tel: (305) 576-2898
Fax: (305) 576-2899

Peter Wooding, FIDSA, ASID
Peter Wooding Design Associates
369 Ives Street
Providence, Rhode Island 02906
Tel: (401) 454-1744
Fax: (401) 751-3896

Alison Wright, AIA
Alison Wright Architects
8800 Venice Boulevard
Los Angeles, California 90034
Tel: (310) 559-7467
Fax: (310) 559-2250

Otto Zapf
Main Road
Post Office Box 842
Orient, New York 11957
Tel: (516) 323-3972
Fax: (516) 323-3996
[See also *Germany*]

Austria

Coop Himmelblau
(Wolf D. Prix and Helmut Swiczinsky)
Seilerstätte 16/11a
A-1010 Vienna
Tel: (43) 1-512 0284-0
Fax: (43) 1-513 47 54-21

Brazil

Arthur de Mattos Casas
Casas Ediçoes de Design
Alameda Casa Branca, 1136, CEP 01408
Sao Paulo, S.P. 01408-000
Tel: (55) 11-282-6311
Fax: (55) 11-282-6608

Canada

Margaret-Lindsay Holton
M.L.H. Productions
98 Margueretta Street
Toronto, Ontario M6H 3S3
Tel: (416) 537-9327
Fax: (416) 922-2230

Denmark

Nanna Ditzel, IDD, FCSD
Klareboderne 4
DK-1115 Copenhagen K.
Tel: (45) 33 93 94 80
Fax: (45) 33 33 94 80

England

Ron Arad
Ron Arad Associates Ltd.
62 Chalk Farm Road
London NW1 8AN
Tel: (44) 71 284 4965
Fax: (44) 71 379 0499

Mark Brazier-Jones, BA (Hons)
Hyde Hall Barn
Buckland Buntingford
Herts. SG9 0RU
Tel: (44) 76 327 3599
Fax: (44) 76 327 3410

Eva Jiricna
Eva Jiricna Architects Limited
7 Dering Street
London W1R 9AB
Tel: (44) 71 629 7077
Fax: (44) 71 491 3370

Finland

Eero Aarnio
Lamminpääntie 26
SF-02880 Veikkola
Tel: 358-0-265 365
Fax: 358-0-268 547

Yrjö Kukkapuro
Studio Kukkapuro
Alppitie 23
00270 Kauniainen
Tel: 358-0-505 1618
Fax: 358-0-505 2251

Antti Nurmesniemi, Professor, HonRDI
Hopeasalmentie 27
00570 Helsinki
Tel: 358 (9) 0-684 7056
Fax: 358 (9) 0-684 8325

Juhani Pallasmaa Architect
    SAFA, Hon. FAIA
Professor
Arkkitehtitoimisto Juhani Pallasmaa Ky
Tehtaankatu 13 B 28
00140 Helsinki
Tel: 358 (9) 0-699 740
Fax: 358 (9) 0-669 741

France

Christian Astuguevieille
Eurl. Astuguevieille
10, rue Portalis
F-75008 Paris
Tel: (33) 1 429 40008
Fax: (33) 1 429 38031

Pucci De Rossi
23 Passage du Nord
92240 Malakoff
Tel: (33) 1 925 30145
Fax: (33) 1 465 66942

Garouste & Bonetti
(Elizabeth Garouste and Mattia Bonetti)
1 rue Oberkampf
75011 Paris
Tel/Fax: (33) 1 480 58651

Jean-Pierre Heim, Architecte D.P.L.G.
Jean-Pierre Heim & Associates, Inc. and
    Design Connection International
24, rue Vieille du Temple
75004 Paris
Tel: (33) 1 488 70708
Fax: (33) 1 427 70181
[See also *United States*]

Andrée Putman
ECART
111, rue Saint-Antoine
75004 Paris
Tel: (33) 1 427 88835
Fax: (33) 1 427 88734

Germany

Otto Zapf
Zapf Design
Herzog-Adolph-Strasse 5
61462 Känigstein
Tel: (49) 6174 7391
Fax: (49) 6174 4975
[See also *United States*]

Hong Kong

John Chan
John Chan Design Ltd.
5/F World-Wide Commercial Building
34 Wyndham Street, Central
Tel: (852) 5210050
Fax: (852) 5267425

Dr. Tao Ho
Taoho Design Architects
Upper Deck
North Point (West) Passenger Ferry Pier
North Point
Tel: (852) 8118780
Fax: (852) 8110337

Italy

Antonia Astori
Antonia Astori Studio di
Architettura & Design
Via Rossini 3
20122 Milan
Tel: (39) 2-795005
Fax: (39) 2-76021763

Anna Castelli Ferrieri, Dott. Arch.
Corsa de Porta Romana 87/B
20122 Milan
Tel: (39) 2-5510451
Fax: (39) 2-551-95715

Antonio Citterio
Studio Citterio Dwan
Via Lovanio, 8
I-20121 Milan
Tel: (39) 2-6555902
Fax: (39) 2-6551303

Paolo Favaretto
Studio Favaretto
Via Gabriele Falloppio, 39
35121 Padova
Tel: (39) 4-98762876
Fax: (39) 4-98762777

Dr. Gianfranco Frattini
Via S. Agnese 14
20123 Milan
Tel: (39) 2-86452378 or 865585
Fax: (39) 2-72021103

Afra and Tobia Scarpa
Via Pilastroni
31040 Trevignano (TV)
Tel: (39) 4-23670092
Fax: (39) 4-23670105

Ettore Sottsass, Jr.
Via Melone, 2
20121 Milan
Tel: (39) 2-86441 or 876306
Fax: (39) 2-809596

George J. Sowden
Studio Sowden
Corso Di Porta Nuova 46
20121 Milan
Tel: (39) 2-653758
Fax: (39) 2-6570228

Transit Design SLR
(Giovanni Ascarelli, Maurizio Macciocchi,
Evaristo Nicolao, Danilo Parisio)
Via Emilio Morosini, 17
00153 Rome
Tel: (39) 6-5899893
Fax: (39) 6-5899894

Japan

Toshiyuki Kita
I.D.K.
2nd Floor, TS Building
3-1-2 Tenma
Kita-ku, Osaka
Tel: (81) 6 357 1525
Fax: (81) 6 357 1529

*Dr. Kisho Kurokawa, Hon. FAIA, Hon.
FRIBA*
Kisho Kurokawa Architect & Associates
Aoyama Bldg. 11-F.
1-2-3 Kita-Aoyama, Minato
Tokyo
Tel: (81) 3 3404 3481
Fax: (81) 3 3404 6222

Shigeru Uchida
Studio 80
1-17-14 Minami-Aoyama
Minato-ku, Tokyo 107
Tel: (81) 3 3479 5071
Fax: (81) 3 3475 4586

Mexico

Gerard Pascal and Carlos Pascal
Pascal Arquitectos
Altaltunco #99
San Miguel Tecamachalco
C. P. 53970
Naucalpan, Estado de Mexico
Tel: (52) 52942371
Fax: (52) 52948513

Netherlands

Borek Sípek
Studio Sípek
Oude Looiersstraat 28
1016 VJ Amsterdam
Tel: (31) 20-6247669
Fax: (31) 20-6233832

Philippines

Antonio (Budji) Layug
Budji Layug Designs
Valgosons Building, Suite 509
2151 Pasong Tamo
Makati, Metro Manila
Tel: (63) 287 6106 81731 43
Fax: (63) 281 0253 8

Spain

Javier Mariscal
Estudio Mariscal
C/Pellaires, n. 30-38
08019 Barcelona
Tel: (34) 3 303 3420
Fax: (34) 3 308 7587

José Luis Pérez Ortega
Urbanizacion Del Golf
Cabo Finesterra, 5-3
28290 Las Matas, Madrid
Tel/Fax: (34) 1 630 0449
[See also *United States*]

Jaime Tresserra
J. Tresserra Design
c/o Josep Bertrand, 17
08021 Barcelona
Tel: (34) 3 200 4922
Fax: (34) 3 200 4734

Oscar Tusquets Blanca
C/Cavallers, n.50
08034 Barcelona
Tel: (34) 3 280 5599
Fax: (34) 3 280 4071

Switzerland

Mario Botta
via Ciani 16
6904 Lugano
Tel: (41) 91 5286 25 or 26 or 27
Fax: (41) 91 5314 54

Manufacturers/Distributors/
Producers

Adelta Oy
c/o Finland Contact GmbH
Friedrich-Ebert-Str.96
D-46535 Dinslaken 1
Germany
Tel: (49 0) 2064-12877
Fax: (49 0) 2064-70229

Agnes Bourne, Inc.
Showplace Design Center
Two Henry Adams Street
Showroom 220
San Francisco, California 94103
United States
Tel: (415) 626-6883
Fax: (415) 626-2489

Akaba, s.a.
c/Mayor S/N
Lasarte, Gipuzkoa
Spain
Tel: (34) 43 37 22 11
Fax: (34) 43 37 10 52

*Alcasar Terrell Environmental
Design Group*
119½ North Larchmont Boulevard
Los Angeles, California 90004
United States
Tel: (213) 469-8044

Alias Spa
Via Leonardo da Vinci, 27
I-20064 Grumello del Monte (BG)
Italy
Tel: (39) 35 44 02 40
Fax: (39) 35 44 09 96

Alison Wright Architects
8800 Venice Boulevard
Los Angeles, California 90034
United States
Tel: (310) 559-7467
Fax: (310) 559-2250

Amat SA
Camino Can Bros 5
08750 Martorell
Barcelona
Spain
Tel: (34) 775 5651
Fax: (34) 775 3454

Andreu World SA
Camino de los Modones
46970 Alacuas
Valencia
Spain

Archetype Gallery
115 Mercer Street
New York, New York 10012
United States
Tel: (212) 334-0100
Fax: (212) 226-7880

Artespaña
Velazquez 140
28006 Madrid
Spain
Tel: (34) 91 561 4339
Fax: (34) 91 563 1235

*Atelier International, Ltd. A Division of
Steelcase Inc. (see Stow & Davis)*
305 East 63rd Street
New York, New York 10021
United States
Tel: (212) 223-7449
Fax: (212) 980-3455

Avarte Oy
Export Office
Hiekkakiventie 2
00710 Helsinki
Finland
Tel: (358) 0 374 2235
Fax: (358) 0 378 112

B.D. Ediciones de Diseño
C/Mallorca, 291
08037 Barcelona
Spain
Tel: (34) 3 458 6909
Fax: (34) 3 207 3697

Bernhardt
Box 740
Lenoir, North Carolina 28645
United States
Tel: (704) 758-9811
Fax: (704) 754-0321

Betty M Showroom
Space 1684 Merchandise Mart
Chicago, Illinois 60654
United States
Tel: (312) 828-0340
Fax: (312) 828-0340

Bradford Stewart & Company
Post Office Box 1672
Palo Alto, California 94302
United States
Tel: (415) 325-4622
Fax: (415) 324-0259

Brayton International, Inc.
255 Swathmore Avenue
High Point, North Carolina 27264
United States
Tel: (919) 434-4240
Fax: (919) 434-4240

Mark Brazier-Jones
Hyde Hall Barn
Buckland Buntingford
Herts SG9 0RU
England
Tel: (44) 76 327 3599
Fax: (44) 76 327 3410

Brueton Industries, Inc.
145-68 228th Street
Springfield Gardens, New York 11413
United States
Tel: (718) 527-3000
Fax: (718) 712-6783

The Budji Collections, Inc.
Valgosons Building, Suite 509
2151 Pasong Tamo
Makati, Metro Manila
Philippines
Tel: (63) 2 8761 06 817 31 43
Fax: (63) 2 8102 53 8

Cannon/Bullock
8407 Melrose Place
Los Angeles, California 90069
United States
Tel: (213) 651-2875
Fax: (213) 651-2876 (call first)

Carlos Jané Camacho
Apartado 243,
08400 Grandollers-Ctra. N-152 Km.
24.100 Barcelona
Spain
Tel: (34) 3 9 93 849-11-65
Fax: (34) 3 9 93 840-00-60

Casas Mobilplast
Poligono Santa Rita
S.L. Apdo. de Correos 1333
08755 Castellbisbal, Barcelona
Spain
Tel: (34) 3 9 772-08-59
Fax: (34) 3 9 772-21-30

Cassina s.p.a.
Via L. Busnelli 1
20036 Meda (MI)
Italy
Tel: (39) 0362-3721
Fax: (39) 0362-340959

Chairs
Axis Bldg. 4F
5-17-1 Roppongi, Minato-ku
Tokyo 106
Japan
Tel: (81) 3-3587-2580
Fax: (81) 3-3582-1280

Clodagh Design Works
365 First Avenue
New York, New York 10010
United States
Tel: (212) 673-9202
Fax: (212) 614-9125

Conde House
2 Henry Adams Street, Suite 291
San Francisco, California 94103
United States
Tel: (415) 864-8666
Fax: (415) 864-5373

Consonni
Via Rienti, 27
22060 Cantu Asnago (CO)
Italy
Tel: (39) 31-706139
Fax: (39) 31-705665

Cy Mann International
Decorative Arts Center
305 East 63rd Street, 6th Floor
New York, New York 10021
United States
Tel: (212) 758-6830
Fax: (212) 758-6735

Dakota Jackson, Inc.
306 East 61st Street
New York, New York 10021
United States
Tel: (212) 838-9444
Fax: (212) 758-6413

Design Connection International
24, rue Vieille du Temple
75004 Paris
France
Tel: (33) 1 48 87 07 08
Fax: (33) 1 42 77 01 81

Designer Imports Ltd.
8th Floor
34 Wyndham Street
Hong Kong
Tel: (852) 1 0060
Fax: (852) 5 9197

Design Trade
c/o Zapf Design
Herzog-Adolph-Strabe 5
D-61462 Königstein
Germany
Tel: (49) 6174 7391
Fax: (49) 6174 4975

Dhana Solish Design
Pacific Design Center-G178
8687 Melrose Avenue
Los Angeles, California 90069
United States
Tel: (310) 652-2015
Fax: (310) 652-0316

Diva
8801 Beverly Boulevard
Los Angeles, California 90048
United States
Tel: (310) 278-3191
Fax: (310) 274-7189

Donghia Furniture
485 Broadway
New York, New York 10013
United States
Tel: (212) 925-2777
Fax: (212) 925-4819

Driade
Via Padana Inferiore, 12
29012 Fossadello di Caorso (PC)
Italy
Tel: (39) 52 3818618
Fax: (39) 52 3822628

Edward David Nieto Design Group, Inc.
108 North East 39th Street
Miami, Florida 33137
United States
Tel: (305) 573-9555
Fax: (305) 573-2255

E.N.T Enterprises, Inc.
8479 Steller Drive
Culver City, California 90232
United States
Tel: (310) 202-6162
Fax: (310) 202-6706

Enza Inc.
420 West 24th Street
New York, New York 10011
United States
Tel: (212) 463-8925
Fax: (212) 366-1715
also
2421 Lake Pancoast Drive
Miami Beach, Florida 33140
United States
Tel: (305) 531-8122
Fax: (305) 531-7726
and
27 Harley Street
London W1N 1DA
England
Tel: (44) 71-637-0798
Fax: (44) 71-637-0795

Estel s.p.a.
via S. Rosa, 70
36016 Thiene, Vicenza
Italy
Tel: (39) 0445-389511
Fax: (39) 0445-370290

Ergo Design Works
8112½ West Third Street, Suite D
Los Angeles, California 90048
United States
Tel: (213) 658-8901
Fax: (213) 658-8903

Estudio Mariscal
c/ Pellaires, n. 30-38
08019 Barcelona
Spain
Tel: (34) 3 303 34 20
Fax: (34) 3 308 7587

EWE-Küchen
Dieselstr. 4
4601 Wels
Austria
Tel: (43) 7242-23733 or 23788
Fax: (43) 7242-23748

Fantoni s.p.a.
Zona Industriale
33010 Osoppo (Udine)
Tel: 0432/9761
Fax: 0432/986246

Frewil Inc.
605 North La Brea Avenue
Los Angeles, California 90036
United States
Tel: (213) 934-8474
Fax: (213) 857-1916

The Gallery
Keizer-Kazel
Plein 8
Maastricht
The Netherlands
Tel: (31) 43 257450
Fax: (31) 43 257178

Garden Follies
7512 Old Bee Cave Road
Austin, Texas 78735
United States
Tel/Fax: (512) 288-2096

Gandy/Peace, Inc.
3195 Paces Ferry Place, Northwest
Atlanta, Georgia 30305-1307
United States
Tel: (404) 237-8681
Fax: (404) 237-6150

Geiger International
7005 Fulton Industrial Boulevard
Atlanta, Georgia 30336
United States
Tel: (404) 344-1100
Fax: (404) 346-5202

Geoffrey Scott Design Associates
Post Office Box 554
Venice, California 90294
United States
Tel/Fax: (310) 396-5416

Gilbert International
459 South Calhoun
Fort Worth, Texas 76104
United States
Tel: (817) 921-5331
Fax: (817) 927-8655

Goodman Charlton
1500 Rising Glen Road
Los Angeles, California 90069
United States
Tel: (310) 657-7068
Fax: (310) 657-1868

Goralnick • Buchanan A&D, Inc.
2109 Broadway, Suite 1492
New York, New York, 10023-2130
United States
Tel: (212) 362-7217
Fax: (212) 362-7254

HaRry
8738 West Third Street
Los Angeles, California 90048
United States
Tel: (310) 550-1555
Fax: (310) 559-3387

HBF
Hickory Business Furniture
Post Office Box 8
Hickory, North Carolina 28603
United States
Tel: (704) 328-2064
Tel: (704) 328-8816

H. Dolin Stuart Inc.
8450 Melrose Place
Los Angeles, California 90069
United States
Tel: (213) 655-3995
Fax: (213) 655-1829

Heinz & Company, Inc.
120 Callan Avenue
Evanston, Illinois 60202
United States
Tel/Fax: (708) 328-6552

Holly Hunt, Ltd.
1728 Merchandise Mart
Chicago, Illinois 60654
United States
Tel: (312) 661-1900
Fax: (312) 661-0243

ICF
International Contract Furnishings
305 East 63rd Street
New York, New York 10021
United States
Tel: (212) 750-0900
Fax: (212) 593-1152

Jack Lenor Larsen, Inc.
41 East 11th Street
New York, New York 10003
United States
Tel: (212) 674-3993
Fax: (212) 674-1403

JANUS et Cie.
Pacific Design Center
8687 Melrose Avenue, B146
West Hollywood, California 90069
United States
Tel: (310) 652-7090
Fax: (310) 652-7928

Jerry Pair & Associates
351 Peachtree Hills Avenue
Suite 508
Atlanta, Georgia 30305
United States
Tel: (800) 367-7247
Fax: (404) 261-0795

J. Robert Scott & Associates, Inc.
8727 Melrose Avenue
Los Angeles, California 90069-5086
United States
Tel: (310) 659-4910
Fax: (310) 842-9513

J. Tresserra Design
c/ Josep Bertrand, 17
08021 Barcelona
Spain
Tel: (34) 3 200 4922
Fax: (34) 3 200 4734

Juan Montoya Furniture and
  Accessories
80 Eighth Avenue
New York, New York 10011
United States
Tel: (212) 242-3622
Fax: (212) 242-3743

Kartell, s.p.a.
Via delle Industrie 1
20082 Binasco, Milan
Italy
Tel: (39) 2 900121
Fax: (39) 2 9053316

The Knoll Group
105 Wooster Street
New York, New York 10012
United States
Tel: (212) 343-4000
Fax: (212) 343-4180

Laurie Ann Clemans Design
1248 Homestead Avenue
Walnut Creek, California 94598
United States
Tel/Fax: (510) 938-3224

Lenny Steinberg Design Associates
1802 Angelo Drive
Beverly Hills, California 90210
United States
Tel/Fax: (310) 271-7870

Limn
290 Townsend
San Francisco, California 94133
United States
Tel: (415) 397-7475
Fax: (415) 543-5971

Mimi London
Pacific Design Center
8687 Melrose Avenue
Los Angeles, California 90069
United States
Tel: (310) 855-2567
Fax: (310) 855-0213

M.L.H. Productions
98 Margueretta Street
Toronto, Ontario M6H 3S3
Canada
Tel: (416) 537-9327
Fax: (416) 922-2230

The Manheim Companies
13736 Beta Road
Dallas, Texas 754244
United States
Tel: (800) 327-1624
Fax: (214) 387-4580

Memphis
Via Olivetti 9
20010 Pregnana, Milan
Italy
Tel: (39) 2 93290663
Fax: (39) 2 93591202

Meritalia S.p.A. Furniture
Via Como, 76/78
22066 Mariano Comense (Como)
Italy
Tel: (39) 031/743100
Fax: (39) 031/744460

MSDS Designs
122 Powers Avenue
Santa Barbara, California 93103
United States
Tel: (805) 963-2234
Fax: (805) 963-0028

Mueller Turner Company
Post Office Box 549
Morongo Valley, California 92256
United States
Tel: (619) 363-6229
Fax: (619) 363-6872

Neotu Gallery
25 rue de Renard
75004 Paris
France
Tel: (33) 1-42 78 91 83
Fax: (33) 1-42 78 96 97
and
84 Wooster Street
New York, New York 10012
United States
Tel: (212) 343-1001
Fax: (212) 343-1015

Noel Jeffrey, Inc.
215 East 58th Street
New York, New York 10022
United States
Tel: (212) 935-7775
Fax: (212) 935-8280

The Pace Collection
11-11 34th Avenue
Long Island City, New York 11106
United States
Tel: (718) 718-8201
Fax: (718) 274-5530

Portobelo Collection
Calle 85 #11-64
Bogota
Colombia
Tel: (57) 1-256-4597
Fax: (57) 1-257-4959

Preview Furniture Corp.
300 Fraley Road
High Point, North Carolina 27261
United States
Tel: (919) 887-3024

Puulon Oy
17800 Kuhmoinen
Finland
Tel: (358) 19-51555
Fax: (358) 19-51556

Puusepänliike Nurmi
Rakentajantie 25
Kaarina 20780
Finland
Tel: (358) 21-2435111
Fax: (358) 21-2433372

Randolph & Hein, Inc.
1 Arkansas Street
San Francisco, California
United States
Tel: (415) 864-3371
Fax: (415) 864-2185

Reimann Mikami, Inc.
720 Iwilei Road, Suite 402
Honolulu, Hawaii 96817-5030
United States
Tel: (808) 538-6836
Fax: (808) 533-7589

Richard Himmel Antique &
  Decorative Furniture
1800 Merchandise Mart Plaza
Chicago, Illinois 60654
United States
Tel: (312) 527-5700
Fax: (312) 527-2169

Ronn Jaffe Incorporated
The Design Studio Building
9204 Harrington Drive
Potomac, Maryland 20854
United States
Tel: (301) 365-3500
Fax: (301) 365-3157

A. Rudin
Pacific Design Center #G980
8687 Melrose Avenue
Los Angeles, California 90069
United States
Tel: (310) 659-2388
Fax: (310) 659-1304

Sandra Nunnerly, Inc.
112 East 71st Street
New York, New York 10021
United States
Tel: (212) 472-9341
Fax: (212) 472-9346

Sherle Wagner International
60 East 57th Street
New York, New York 10022
United States
Tel: (212) 758-3300
Fax: (212) 207-8010

Sottass Associati
Via Melone, 2
20121 Milan
Italy
Tel: (39) 2-86441 or 876306
Fax: (39) 2-809596

Spinneybeck Design America
45 Hazelwood Drive
Amherst, New York 14228
United States
Tel: (716) 691-2840
Fax: (716) 691-2823

Stansson Studio
2318 Northeast Second Court
Miami, Florida 33137-4506
United States
Tel: (305) 576-2898
Fax: (305) 576-2899

Fredericia Stolefabrik
Treldevej 183
DK-7000 Fredericia
Denmark
Tel: (45) 7592 3344
Fax: (45) 7592 3876

Stow & Davis/A Division of
  Steelcase Inc.
4300 44th Street
Grand Rapids, Michigan 49512
United States
Tel: (616) 247-2710
Fax: (616) 698-1522

Strassle Sohne & Co.
Postcheck 90-5033-4
Station Bazenhead
AG 9533 Kirchberg SG
Switzerland
Tel: (41) 73-312631
Fax: (41) 73-312733

Studio Amerika Limited
504 Armour Circle, NE
Atlanta, Georgia 30324
United States
Tel: (404) 874-4672

Studio Steel by Steven Hensel
2202 North Pacific
Seattle, Washington 98103
United States
Tel: (206) 547-7706

Norman Sukkar Furniture
13 Avenue A
New York, New York 10009
United States
Tel: (212) 477-4477
Fax: (212) 260-1160

Thayer Coggin
230 South Road
Post Office Box 5867
High Point, North Carolina 27262
United States
Tel: (919) 841-6000
Fax: (919) 841-3245

Therien & Co., Inc.
411 Vermont Street
San Francisco, California 94107
United States
Tel: (415) 956-8850
Fax: (415) 861-2192
also
716 North La Cienega Boulevard
Los Angeles, California 90069
United States
Tel: (310) 657-4615
Fax: (310) 657-2819

Tribal Design
1001 East Almeda
Sante Fe, New Mexico 87501
United States
Tel: (505) 989-8765
Fax: (505) 989-3353

UMS Pastoe B.V.
Rotsoord 3
3523 CL Utrecht, Holland
The Netherlands
Tel: (31) 3052-2340
Fax: (31) 3051-2141

Volz Clarke & Associates
One Cottage Street
Easthamptons, Massachusetts 01027
United States
Tel: (413) 527-8656
Fax: (413) 527-0502

The Wicker Works
267 Eighth Street
San Francisco, California
United States
Tel: (415) 626-6730
Fax: (415) 626-8138

Index

Architects and Designers

Manufacturers/Distributors/Producers

Photographers

Acknowledgments

First and above all, I would like to extend my gratitude to Publisher Mark Serchuck and Managing Director Penny Sibal for once again giving me the opportunity to create a book for their fine PBC International, Inc. I also am indebted to Susan Kapsis for accepting the responsibility for this book mid-stream, at which time she was appointed as PBC's managing editor, and for bringing to its pages her intelligent and careful attention. Working hand in hand with her was PBC's Technical Director Richard Liu, upon whose expert analysis we depended entirely. Garrett Schuh's design, sensitive to the subject as well as innovative in its own right, added the dimension for which one yearns when composing a book about the arts.   And bouquets to editorial assistants Francine Hornberger and Debra Harding—so professionally thorough in pursuit of perfection.

The number of people with whom I have been in contact to obtain the materials from more than one hundred design professionals are many, and I am deeply grateful for the assistance of each and every one. Often when interviewing an architect or designer it would be his or her associates who would spend just as much time or more following through with all the details and paperwork. Although I cannot name all of these individuals, I would like to mention a few others who went out of their way in helping me make contact with those architects and designers in the first place:

Roslyn Brandt, *Barnes and Brandt Inc., New York City*
Ken Burrows, *Terra Furniture, City of Industry, California*
Britt L. Carlsson, *Swedish Attaché of Technology, Los Angeles*
Mirja Covarrubias, *Information Service of Finland, Los Angeles*
Olle Furberg, *Sveriges Möbelhandlares Centralförbund, Stockholm, Sweden*
Vivien Harrison, *Uniquely Australian Corp., Victoria, British Columbia*
Lena Torslow Hansen, *Art Consulting: Scandinavia, Calabasas, California*
Akira Hashimoto, *Nihon Sekkei U.S.A., Inc., Los Angeles*
George Johnson, *Atelier International, Inc., Long Island City, New York*
Andrew Ma, *Hong Kong Development Council, Hong Kong*
Joyce May, *British Consulate General, Los Angeles*
Michael Merritt, *Whitney, Inc., Chicago*
Lisa Pierce, *Italian Trade Commission, Atlanta, Georgia*
Cheryl L. Ruine, *Ruine Design Associates, New York*
Brigitta Schoch, *Deputy Consul General, Consulate General of Switzerland, Los Angeles*
Jean-Claude Terrac, *Cultural Attaché, French Consulate, Los Angeles*
Marcia Van Liew, *Lawrence & Scott, Seattle, Washington*
Christina Villo, *Procova, Los Angeles*
Ben Watson, *Vitra Seating, Inc., Long Island City, New York*